I saw Jason for the first time after he had just been admitted to acute inpatient rehabilitation. At that time, he was unable to move his arms or legs. Then there was a muscle twitch, which began his incredible road to recovery. Day after day he persevered and overcame the many obstacles that life had placed before him. He relearned to do the things that many of us take for granted, including eating, dressing, and walking. Jason struggled to retake control of his life and fought against a system that is not friendly for those with disabilities. It is with tenacity for life, justice, his family, and his belief in a higher power that kept his will to live when many others may have quit. We are extremely proud of Jason!

—Dr. Jeffrey Berliner, DO, TIRR Memorial Hermann

I had the pleasure of meeting Jason while he was a patient at Texas Institute for Rehabilitation and Research (TIRR). I remember him being in a wheelchair, wearing a neck brace, and constantly having an entourage of uniformed officers in his presence. Jason always had what seemed like an amazingly overwhelming aura of positive energy, which is very rare to see in a patient who has sustained such life-altering injuries. It wasn't until we started working together at Kirby Glen that I began to personally know the incredibly strong-willed, awe-inspiring man that he is. The fight that Jason has put up is absolutely remarkable. This is a man who was initially told that he would never walk again. Just saying this gives me the chills! Not only did Jason walk, he ran—sprinted, actually! And faster than me! Day after day, week after week, Jason would sweat, moan, groan, fall down, get back up, wipe himself off, and say *"Let's go!"* with a smile and a look of determination on his face. I have never, in my professional career as a physical therapist, had the opportunity and honor to work with a man who has shown that *nothing* will keep him down. It is because of Jason that I am humbled and grateful I can go to work every day. Thank you for that, Jason! You are truly an inspiration!

—Wendy Brown, PT, DPT, TIRR Memorial Herman

I have never seen anyone suffer the types of injuries that Jason has endured all at the same time. Sustaining a spinal cord injury, brain injury, and a stroke usually ends with debilitating outcomes. For Jason, these were mere speed bumps to where he stands now. He is the definition of determination, perseverance, and most important ... faith! His faith in God has led him to inspire many people, including myself. I had the privilege to treat someone who was giving, caring, and hardworking. Jason is a walking miracle.

—Jonathan Parr, PT, MCMT, CBIS, HFS, Spero Rehab

I've only had the pleasure of knowing Jason since the time of his injury, but I feel like I've known him a lifetime. Jason is an absolute incredible human being and nothing short of a walking miracle. The severities of Jason's injuries were so complex that it was thought that his recovery would be minimal at best. Jason's nonstop work, headstrong determination, and faith in God are the only explanation for his miraculous recovery. Jason learned not only to be an advocate for himself in his fight against the system, but how to persevere against all odds and beat something that seemed to be much bigger than him. Most people do not have the fight in them to get through this, but Jason's recovery, which I have had the honor of treating and seeing firsthand, is a true testament to faith, hope, and will to survive.

—Katie Bouchillon, OTR, ATP, CBIS, Owner/ Clinical Director, Spero Rehabilitation, LLC

# FROM
# ZERO TO
# A HUNDRED

## FINDING MY PURPOSE THROUGH MY PAIN

## JASON ROY

WESTBOW®
PRESS
A DIVISION OF THOMAS NELSON
& ZONDERVAN

WestBow Press books may be ordered through booksellers or by contacting:
WestBow Press
A Division of Thomas Nelson & Zondervan
1663 Liberty Drive
Bloomington, IN 47403
www.westbowpress.com
1 (866) 928-1240

Because of the dynamic nature of the Internet, any web addresses or
links contained in this book may have changed since publication and
may no longer be valid. The views expressed in this work are solely those
of the author and do not necessarily reflect the views of the publisher,
and the publisher hereby disclaims any responsibility for them.

All Bible verses from Chapters 1–16 were taken from The Student Bible,
New International Version by Zondervan Publishing House, 1996.
The salvation prayer in Chapter 16 was taken from
www.salvationprayer.info/prayer.html.

Photo credit by: Touché Harvey at Touché Studios.
www.touchestudios.com
5804 Star Ln, suite B
Houston, Tx 77057
Office: 713-370-4400

Any people depicted in stock imagery provided by Thinkstock are models,
and such images are being used for illustrative purposes only.
Certain stock imagery © Thinkstock.

ISBN: 978-1-4908-3209-8 (sc)
ISBN: 978-1-4908-3208-1 (hc)
ISBN: 978-1-4908-3210-4 (e)

Library of Congress Control Number: 2014905798

Printed in the United States of America.

WestBow Press rev. date: 6/13/2014

*It's not about what you accomplish at the end of the day; it's about what you overcome when faced with adversity.*

—Robin Roberts, American television broadcaster, winner of the 2013 Arthur Ashe Courage Award

# CONTENTS

# INTRODUCTION

"For I know the plans I have for you," declares the Lord, "plans to prosper you and not harm you, plans to give you hope and a future."

Jeremiah 29:11

This book is an unveiling of my life story. It is my testimony about the things I've experienced that have redefined my character and redirected my path so that I may glorify God in everything I do.

I never imagined I would have to lose what I thought was the life of my dreams to begin living my true destiny. I was a five-year veteran of the Houston Police Department responsible for numerous felony arrests, eighteen commendations, and a unit citation from the chief of police. I was on top of the world. I was consumed with working long hours and accumulating as much financial wealth as possible, as that was how I defined success at the time.

I was fearless, and I truly believed I was invincible. I was living life according to my plans, not God's will. On May 3, 2011, I was involved in a high-speed chase that ended with my squad car flipping multiple times before landing in a ditch. The impact of the collision was so severe that I was trapped inside and had to be extracted from the car. I'm not sure exactly how long I was stuck, but it seemed like an eternity. I was covered in my own blood as I sat there suffocating and nearly choking to death. Then I heard a voice say, "You're about to die. Get ready—you're about to die." My life flashed before me in an instant, and I immediately thought about who would raise my son and take care of my family. Dying at thirty-two years old was not a part of my plan. I desperately wanted to live so that I could be there for my son and family, but I knew the odds were stacked against me. This wasn't my first near-fatal automobile accident, and I honestly didn't think God would spare my life again.

Obviously I am still alive, but the road to recovery has been long and filled with adversity and uncertainty. I've had multiple surgeries, suffered a major stroke, and was paralyzed from the neck down. I couldn't walk, talk, or breathe on my own. I was fighting for my life, and the things I had once taken for granted I now needed to survive. I was afraid, helpless, and powerless. I was forced to rely on other people for everything. I was living my worst nightmare. I was a prisoner in my own body. I often wondered, *Will things ever be the same? How do I pick up the pieces and rebuild my life?* I didn't know how I would do it, but I quickly realized that the first step in recovery was letting go of my plans and submitting to God's will. I knew it wasn't going to be easy, but I truly believed that if I put my faith and trust in God, He would take my life from zero to one hundred.

# PREFACE

I wrote this book because I know it is my duty to share my testimony to inspire and encourage others in hopes that my story will help draw them closer to God. This book is about the circumstances of my life, both good and bad, the seemingly insurmountable adversity I've overcome, and the changes I've made since realizing and accepting God's plan for me. But the idea for the book began years before I knew I would write it. It began when I was lying in a hospital bed, paralyzed and depressed and asking myself one question: How do I recover now that I've hit rock bottom and it seems like I've lost it all?

This book isn't about the time it takes a sports car to accelerate from zero to one hundred miles per hour. It is about being at your lowest point in life, finding your inner strength, and trusting that God will use whatever adversity you may encounter to help you discover your purpose in life.

During my childhood, my mother taught me that life is a series of hurdles and adjustments. In retrospect I can appreciate all the setbacks I've experienced, because they have helped shape my character and strengthen my faith. But it wasn't so easy to accept during my darkest moments. It wasn't until I submitted myself to God and put my entire faith in His hands that I understood that everything happens for a reason. Now I know that the obstacles we encounter and the situations we perceive as accidents are actually all part of God's plans for our lives. It is imperative for you to know that everything that happens to you, including the unexpected problems, happen for a reason and will ultimately help you reach your destiny. Accepting this has allowed me to appreciate my own personal struggles.

My journey in getting back to one hundred percent isn't complete; however, God has given me a message and personal testimony to share and build a relational bridge so that He can walk across my heart to yours. I've written this book to share some of the lessons I've learned as well as the mistakes I've made. It is my prayer that this book will encourage you to discover your true identity and purpose in life, and develop a stronger relationship with Jesus Christ. I hope you will allow this book to come into your life and touch your spirit. Let this be a true testament of God's greatness.

 # 1 DEAD ON ARRIVAL

And we know that all things God works for the good of those who love him, who have been called according to his purpose. For those God foreknew he also predestined to be conformed to the likeliness of his Son, that he might be the firstborn among many brothers. And those he predestined, he also called: those he called, he also justified; those he justified, he also glorified.

—Romans 8:28–30

The paramedics arrived on the scene of the accident and found my lifeless, fifteen year old body lying in the street. They quickly determined I didn't have a pulse and unofficially pronounced me DOA—dead on arrival. They covered my body with a white sheet and began attending to the other passengers involved in the wreck. I don't recall many of the details of the crash, but it's my understanding that I was unconscious for several minutes. In the midst of all the commotion I woke up, pulled the sheet off my face, and was blinded by all the flashing lights from the ambulances and fire trucks. It was the beginning of a series of events that would eventually lead me to my ultimate destiny. I don't remember seeing a light at the end of a tunnel or having an out of body experience, but I do recall being very disoriented. I didn't know where I was or what had happened to me; I was just grateful to be alive.

On July 10, 1994, the summer before my sophomore year in high school, I was involved in a car accident that nearly claimed my life. It started out like any other ordinary day. I was following my normal routine of working out and spending time with my friends. That afternoon a few of my friends, teammates and I learned we had been selected to play on a private all-star baseball team. After receiving the good news, we decided to go to the movies to celebrate. After we left the movies, I called my dad and asked if I could spend the night at my friend Derrick's house. Initially my dad said I couldn't stay, but he reluctantly gave in after listening to several minutes of me begging and pleading my case. As soon as I arrived at Derrick's house, his father agreed to drive us to the grocery store to grab a few snacks for the game the next day. I had no idea that what started as an ordinary car ride to the store would change my life forever.

I jumped into the rear passenger seat of the Jeep Cherokee and decided not to put my seat belt on. The store was right around the corner, and it didn't seem like a big deal at the time. Unfortunately, we never made it to the store. A few minutes into the drive we were blindsided by a drunk driver. It is believed that the car that struck us was going at least a hundred miles per hour. The impact was so powerful that it caused the Jeep to flip over multiple times. Because I was not wearing my seat belt, I was thrown several feet and landed in the middle of a busy intersection. Derrick and his dad remained inside the truck, and I was lying alone in the street.

The sounds of the crash caused a man who lived near the scene to awaken from his sleep and rush to our aid. I don't know if I would have survived if he had not reacted so quickly. He told his wife to call the police and stood in front of me as I lay motionless on the ground, protecting my body from oncoming traffic. I was later told that the man was having a nightmare about a horrible car accident. He woke up to tell his wife about his dream and she told him to go back to sleep. Fortunately for us he trusted his instincts and looked out the window just to be sure that it was in fact a dream. He was shocked to find that what he thought was a vivid figment of his imagination was actually staring him in the face.

Derrick's father was eventually able to climb out of the truck and escaped with only minor cuts and bruises. Derrick was trapped inside the car and had to be removed by the paramedics and firemen. He also suffered a head injury and was in a coma for several days. One of the most difficult parts of the entire ordeal was that my friend and I were separated. We were placed in two different ambulances and sent to two different hospitals, so I wasn't able to see him again for several weeks.

When I arrived at the hospital, paramedics raced through the hospital doors and took me directly to the emergency room, where a trauma response team awaited my arrival. They were suited up like highly skilled soldiers ready for combat, and the war they were fighting was one to save my life. As soon as the paramedics transferred me from the stretcher to the hospital bed, the doctors and nurses swarmed the bed and started their initial evaluation. They quickly determined that the best course of action was to sedate me and put me on life support so they could continue to evaluate my injuries and begin the appropriate next level of care.

While I was sedated, they took several CT scans of my head, chest, and limbs. The scans revealed a host of life-threatening injuries. I had generalized brain swelling with a focal injury, which was most likely caused by the impact of the crash before I was ejected from the Jeep. The right side of my pelvis was shattered, both of my legs were broken, and my lungs were unstable and on the verge of collapsing. The doctors were extremely concerned about the swelling on my brain. The first few hours were the most critical. They monitored my condition very closely for several hours, looking for signs of permanent brain damage. The doctors did not know if or when I would recover, and they were concerned that they might have to operate on my brain to relieve the pressure caused by the swelling. But God is amazing, and as the days passed, the swelling on my brain subsided significantly, and no surgery was required.

My body lay motionless on the hospital bed. Other than sounds from the machine that was sustaining my life at the lowest level of human existence, there was no indication that I was going to survive. As the days progressed, I slowly began to regain consciousness. I remember the day my eyelids began to flicker and I finally opened my eyes. It took a while to focus. When I was finally able to see my surroundings, I was shocked to find myself lying in a hospital room. Shortly after I woke up, my parents, sister, and other family members and friends entered the room. They were overjoyed that I was finally awake, but I needed time to process exactly what was happening. The questions started racing through my head. Why am I here? How long have I been here? What is wrong with me? As I was having this internal dialogue, I had what at the time seemed like an out-of-body experience. It didn't seem real. I felt like a spectator watching someone else's life. My mind wouldn't allow me to believe this was happening to me. It had to be a nightmare.

I experienced a myriad of emotions the first few days after I regained consciousness. First I was in denial. I refused to believe this was actually happening to me. I had spent the summer preparing for my sophomore year of high school. There was no way that I was lying in a hospital bed, unable to walk and care for myself. It wasn't long before my denial turned to anger. I was angry with everyone about everything. I hated being in the hospital, and it was painfully obvious to my doctors, family, and the hospital staff. After a few days of being mad at the world, I felt myself sinking into a mild depression. I was miserable and inconsolable. The only thing that would have made me happy was walking out of that hospital and going home to return to my old, normal life, the life I formerly knew. Eventually I accepted that I wasn't living a nightmare and that everything that was happening to me was my new reality, and the cramped, cold, white hospital room became my new home.

It was extremely difficult to spend day after day in a hospital bed. I was an active, athletic, energetic, and independent teenage boy, so I hated the monotony of lying on my back, unable to handle the simplest of tasks for myself. I was trapped in my own body, anchored to a hospital bed, connected to more tubes and monitors than I could count. My body was divided into two distinct parts. My upper body, which seemed to be functioning normally, considering the beating it had taken in the accident, and my lower body, which felt completely disconnected and almost nonexistent. I didn't know the extent of my injuries, and I was so overwhelmed that it didn't occur to me to ask why I couldn't move my legs. I questioned my parents and doctors as they gave me the grim prognosis. It was then that I learned that I was only at the beginning of what was going to be a very long recovery process. They told me that as soon as I was stable enough to withstand the move, I would be transferred from Ben Taub's ICU to Texas Children's Hospital for further treatment and observation. The realization of how distant my recovery was sent me into a depression. I felt sorry for myself. I actually didn't even feel like myself. Everything that had previously defined me had been taken away in the blink of an eye. I was no longer the strong, lively athlete I had worked so hard to become, and I definitely didn't identify with the weak, feeble guy lying in this hospital bed. I remained in ICU for the next two weeks before moving on to the next phase of my journey at TCH.

*Front view of Jeep Cherokee in 1994 accident*

*Side view of impact where Jason was sitting*

*Interior view of Jeep Cherokee*

*Rear view of Jeep window where Jason was ejected*

# SECOND CHANCES

Endure hardship as discipline; God is treating you as sons. For what son is not disciplined by his father? If you are not disciplined (and everyone undergoes discipline), then you are illegitimate children and not true sons.

—Hebrews 12:7–8

When I arrived at Texas Children's Hospital, I was greeted by and introduced to my new team of doctors and nurses. As soon as I arrived, they started examining me and assessing my injuries. Not a moment passed that someone didn't come in to check my vitals, draw blood, change my bandages and IV lines, or find some other reason to touch and disturb me. I was in pain and exhausted. I didn't like the attention. I wanted to be a normal kid, but I didn't know if I would ever be the old Jason again. The odds were stacked against me. Every doctor had his own opinion, and none of them were favorable. They told me I would probably never be able to run again, so playing sports was highly unlikely. As I listened to the doctors discuss all of the things I wouldn't be able to do as a result of my injuries, something in my mind and my spirit changed. I traded in my feelings of sadness and depression for motivation and determination. The obstacles in front of me seemed insurmountable, but I was determined to prove the medical experts wrong.

A few weeks into my recovery I started to become curious about the details of my car accident. I didn't remember much, so I asked my father to tell me as much as he could. It was a very emotional conversation. His voice was cracking and he was doing his best not to cry. He said that when he arrived at the scene of the accident, shattered glass was everywhere and the Jeep was flipped upside down in a ditch. The sight of it was so horrible that he thought we were all dead. My dad told me we had been hit by a drunk driver who clearly had no regard for the lives of others, as she had fled the scene on foot. She was an undocumented immigrant who was driving without a license and while under the influence of alcohol. My sister showed me pictures of the Jeep. It was such a mangled mess that I could barely recognize it. It looked like it had been run over by a monster truck. It didn't seem real, but the fact that I had spent the last several weeks in ICU and the hospital was evidence that it was a harsh reality. My side of the Jeep was completely smashed, the roof was caved in, and shattered glass and blood covered the interior. When I looked at the images of the Jeep, I couldn't believe I had survived such a horrible crash. I was also very concerned about my friend Derrick and his father, the other two passengers in the Jeep. My parents had been focused on caring for me, so they didn't know much about how Derrick and his dad were doing. Days later Derrick's dad stopped by my room to check on my progress and give me an update on Derrick's condition. He had escaped the accident with minor cuts and bruises, but Derrick had been in a coma and was just beginning to regain consciousness and open his eyes. I was happy that Derrick was alive, but I was also sad, because I knew he had a painful and lengthy road to recovery ahead of him.

The doctors were prepared to treat and deal with my physical injuries, but none of us expected the behavioral and personality changes I faced. I knew something was a little "off," but I couldn't put my finger on it. My parents noticed the changes in my behavior. I was very irritable, impatient, and quick tempered. The smallest things would set me off and often resulted in me cursing at whoever was the object of my wrath at the time. I don't remember each incident, but my parents said there were a few times that I lashed out physically. I remember getting so upset and frustrated that I punched one of the nurses in the face. I felt bad immediately after I hit her, but I couldn't stop myself, and I didn't know what I was doing. This was a total deviation from my character, so my parents scheduled a meeting with a neurologist to determine the cause and source of my anger and aggression. The doctor determined that my erratic behavior and violent outbursts were likely caused by my brain injury. He explained that I had sustained some damage to my frontal lobe, which controls the executive functions of the brain, such as planning, creating, reasoning, communicating, and problem solving, and as a result I was experiencing neurobehavioral changes. This news was devastating, unexpected, and introduced a new set of challenges to my recovery process.

Before my accident, I was an outgoing, fun, and adventurous teenager. I was full of energy and loved life. After my accident, I felt like a completely different person. My demeanor was aggressive and hostile. I was apathetic toward life and unmotivated to do anything but lie in bed and watch television. I knew I would have to deal with the obvious physical injuries from the accident, but I wasn't prepared for the radical changes in my behavior and personality. I had drastic mood swings and would fly into unexpected rages. One minute I would be calm and content, and the next I'd feel sad, anxious, and depressed. My emotions were out of control. My ability to empathize with others was gone. I was indifferent to everyone and everything around me. I didn't care about myself or anyone else. My attention span decreased dramatically, and I was easily distracted. It was difficult for me to concentrate on anything for more than a few minutes at a time. I also experienced some short-term memory loss. I remember forgetting simple things like my nurses' names and found myself asking the same questions repeatedly. My mind was filled with hundreds of jumbled thoughts, and I couldn't seem to sort through or articulate them clearly. I felt like I was going crazy.

I also experienced physical problems as a result of my head trauma. I was tired all the time. All I wanted to do was lie in bed all day, but when I tried to sleep, I was restless and never managed to actually relax or sleep well. I had random dizzy spells and sometimes had problems speaking and pronouncing words properly. My physical wounds from the accident were healing, but mentally and emotionally I was a wreck. The realization that I would have to rehabilitate my body and my brain was overwhelming. Immediately after the appointment with the neurologist, I started working with specialists to address my brain injuries. They developed a tailored treatment program to meet my needs. Over time I learned coping and problem-solving skills as well as stress-relief techniques to help curb my impulsive behaviors and regulate my emotions. It wasn't easy, but eventually I learned to empathize and relate to others again. I wasn't "cured," but at least I was starting to feel like my old self again.

Rehabilitating my leg (and waiting on my pelvic bone to heal) was an especially long and agonizing process. I had to be kept in a horizontal position at all times until my bones fully healed. The days seemed to drag on as I lay in bed staring at the ceiling. I had never been so bored in my life. I had a tan from the artificial light in the room and was eager to get out of bed and go out into the world again. I wanted to feel the sun on my skin and feel the breeze. I started to understand how much I had taken for granted. I hadn't realized how much of a blessing it was to go for a walk outside until I couldn't walk or go outside on my own. After several weeks of physical therapy, I was still unable to walk and had to use a wheelchair. I was in a lot of pain and felt like I wasn't making any progress. My parents did their best to keep me in good spirits. My dad would take me to McDonald's for an apple pie, and my mom made sure I had plenty of my favorite Popsicles and fruit juices. These treats offered temporary relief from my sadness, but I would eventually fall back into the same cycle of anger, frustration, and depression. I was embarrassed and didn't want anyone to see me in a wheelchair.

My dad constantly reminded me that I was fortunate to be alive and that I shouldn't let my insecurities keep me from enjoying the gift of life. It didn't happen overnight, but I slowly started to appreciate being alive and made a conscious decision that I was not going to let my circumstances define or defeat me. I accepted responsibility for my part in my recovery and vowed to leave the hospital a better, stronger person than I was when I arrived. I also found the courage to face my fears. My dad helped me into my wheelchair and took me for my first walk outside in weeks. It felt amazing!

Three weeks after I arrived at Texas Children's Hospital, X-rays showed that my legs and pelvis had been set long enough for me to attempt to bear my own weight. I was in pain and at times irritable, but I was ready to start the next phase of my recovery. I remember the first day they took me to the hospital gym so I could try to stand for the first time. I was extremely nervous. My legs were wobbling beneath me, and I felt like a toddler learning to stand and walk for the first time. I couldn't stand on my own and felt like a certified weakling. I balanced myself with the help of my physical therapists and the parallel bars for a moment before I retreated back to the safety and security of my wheelchair. I was weak and in pain, but I was determined to walk again. The following morning I was eager to get the day started as I anticipated my trip to the gym. I was committed to walking again and willing to do whatever it took to make it happen.

I used my failures from the previous days and the memories of the past to motivate me to do better. One day while I was lying in bed, I thought about when I played Little League baseball. I could actually see myself at bat, running around the bases, and it reminded me of how fast and graceful I had been on the baseball field. That vision prompted me to push myself past the limit and release an inner strength I didn't know I possessed.

My parents were also instrumental during my rehabilitation process. I could not have done it without their encouraging words, prayers, and unyielding strength. I knew I had a long way to go and that the road would not be easy, but I was devoted to improving each day. Transitioning from the comfort and security of a wheelchair to the uncertainty and independence of walking on my own was a bit intimidating at first. I still needed assistance to walk, but every day I felt myself growing stronger and more confident. I was still in the infancy stage of my re-creation, but I was making significant progress.

As the summer advanced, my hopes of returning to school and playing baseball started to diminish. I was still unable to walk, and I definitely couldn't run, so the prospect of playing sports had gone from a goal to a distant dream. My doctors and parents determined I wasn't healthy enough to attend traditional high school. I had to focus all of my energy and efforts on getting stronger and learning to walk again. Instead of preparing for the first day of school like other kids my age, I was headed to yet another hospital.

# WHY AM I STILL ALIVE?

"I will restore you to health and heal your wounds,"
declares the Lord.

—Jeremiah 30:17

The excitement of completing my tour at Texas Children's Hospital was short lived. The next stop on my journey was the Texas Institute for Rehabilitation and Research, also known as TIRR. At the time, TIRR, an inpatient rehabilitation hospital, was ranked fourth in the country. My physicians were hopeful that working with the physical therapists and staff there would help me recover fully, but I was homesick and dreaded the thought of going to yet another hospital. It had been an excruciating couple of months, and I didn't want to spend one more night away from the comforts of my home. I begged my parents to take me home. I cried, threw temper tantrums, and complained relentlessly. It took me a few days to calm down, but eventually I settled into my new "home" and routine. I loathed being there, but I decided to make the best of it, because I knew that the sooner I got better, the sooner I could go home!

One word sums up how I felt: *frustrated*! I still had to rely on the assistance of others to complete the simplest tasks, such as walking, taking a shower, and getting dressed. Even as a small child I had always been very independent, so it was difficult for me to have to depend on other people to care for me. Feeling like I had very little control over my personal life, coupled with my inability to satisfy my own needs, was very disconcerting. All I wanted to do was be a normal teenager. I wanted to go to regular school, play sports, and hang out with my friends. Those things seemed like reasonable requests, so I couldn't understand why God was punishing me by taking them away. I remember thinking it was just plain unfair that this was happening to me. I kept asking God, "Why me?" Just a few months earlier, I had dedicated myself to being the best athlete I could be. I'd overcome my insecurities, trained hard, and sacrificed an entire summer so I could prove I had what it took to make the baseball team. And just when I had reached my ultimate goal of being selected to play on an all-star team; it was all taken from me in an instant. I felt angry and defeated. I was fifteen years old and too immature to understand the lesson and see God's bigger vision for my life.

I remained at TIRR for approximately three weeks. During that time I followed a strict daily routine. Each morning the nurses would come into my room to check my vitals and give me my medications. After I ate breakfast and got dressed for the day, with the assistance of one of the nurses, I would meet with my physical therapist and attend strength and conditioning classes. The majority of my therapy was focused on rehabilitation exercises and physical therapy to reduce the stiffness and restore movement in my legs.

My hard work and diligence finally paid off. I learned to walk again and was finally on my way home! It had been the longest and most difficult summer of my life, but I was grateful I'd survived and ecstatic to be leaving the hospital and returning to my old life—or so I thought. My parents and I met with my doctors and physical therapists before I was released from TIRR. It was then that I learned I would not return to public school and would be homeschooled. The news crushed me like a ton of bricks. I'd already accepted that I wouldn't be able to immediately rejoin the baseball and basketball teams, but I'd had no idea I was going to be forced to spend my sophomore year of high school stuck in my house.

Although my pelvis and legs had healed enough for me to transition from inpatient rehabilitation to an outpatient program, I still wasn't healthy enough to attend public school. My therapists designed a rigorous schedule that required me to attend therapy three times a week for several hours each session. I was also dealing with the effects of my frontal lobe injury, as I was still more agitated and aggressive than normal. Being homeschooled allowed me to complete my schoolwork around my physical therapy schedule and engage in talk therapy with my tutor. In addition to assisting me with my academic assignments, my tutor was tasked with helping me adapt to basic human behavior, such as regulating my emotions and curbing my impulsive actions. I appreciated her assistance, but I hated being homeschooled. It was extremely boring. I missed the social interaction with my peers and teachers. My days were filled with doctor and physical therapy appointments and sitting alone at my desk working on my school assignments. I didn't have a social life and started to feel isolated from the rest of the world. For months I had longed to go home, but now my life at home was empty and quiet. In some ways it seemed worse than being at the hospital. At least there I could converse and interact with the doctors, other patients, and staff. Spending so much time with myself at home forced me to be alone with my thoughts, which weren't always pleasant. I didn't know if I would ever return to a regular high school setting or even finish school, but in those quiet moments, I was forced to acknowledge that my life was forever changed.

After I settled into my routine at home, I started to reflect on the car accident and how my life had changed as a result. Every time I was alone with my thoughts, I asked myself the same questions: Did I really die that night? Was it God's divine intervention that restored life into my earthly body? Why am I still alive?

The paramedics determined that I was DOA—dead on arrival—a term used to indicate that a person was found already clinically dead upon the arrival of professional medical assistance, such as paramedics. According to the Texas Department of Transportation, fatal injuries from car accidents are the number one cause of death in the United States of America amongst people under the age of thirty-five. Additionally, people who do not wear their seat belts are thirty times more likely to be ejected from a vehicle during a crash, and according to the Centers for Disease Control and Prevention, more than three-fourths of those individuals die from their injuries. Based on this information, I should not have survived such a horrific accident. So why am I still here to share my story?

While I was researching and gathering information for this book, I stumbled across *The Survivors Club,* a book written by Ben Sherwood. The book discusses a survival formula related to automobile accidents and trauma cases. According to the formula, three factors determine whether or not a person will survive the trauma. The first factor is primarily focused on the person's age and the extent of his or her injuries; it is estimated that 85 percent of survival is based on these two variables. The second factor is concerned with the circumstances surrounding the accident or trauma, such as the location of the incident and the nature of medical care the patient receives, since we know some medical institutions and professionals are more sophisticated than others. The third and final factor considers the intangibles that surround the accident and the patient, and pays attention to elements such as the patient's personality, external support system, and spiritual faith. One study showed that patients with optimistic attitudes were likely to live longer than their pessimistic peers. Another study found that a correlation between survival and the number of family members and friends who came to the hospital to support the patient, indicating that patients with larger support systems were more likely to survive and recover than those who had no support. Finally there is a belief that a person's faith and belief in a higher spiritual power can cause them to have a greater chance of survival. Although this goes beyond the realm of medical science and empirical proof, there is a strong consensus that God is real and angels do exist.

I know God was my survival formula on the evening of July 10, 1994. The side of the Jeep on which I was sitting took the bulk of the impact and sustained the most damage before flipping over and landing in a ditch. Investigators told my parents that if I had been wearing my seat belt, I probably would have been crushed and killed instantly. Was this a coincidence? I was ejected from the car and landed in the middle of a busy intersection. What are the odds that I would survive and a stranger would wake up from what he thought was a dream and run into traffic to protect what appeared to be a dead body from oncoming cars? Was this merely another coincidence? The answer is a resounding no! God positioned me right where he wanted me to be and caused others to come to my rescue. He knew that if I had been wearing my seat belt, I would have been crushed. He knew that had that neighbor not been there to shield me from the cars, I probably would have been run over. God lives inside of you and me and wants to see us succeed and fulfill His plans for our lives. During our most difficult times we have to remain faithful and trust God to protect and keep us.

While here on Earth, most of us will experience the death of a loved one or other hardships in our lives. Even the most faithful Christian is not immune from the heartache that is caused by that loss or the devastation of a tragedy. But we should all take comfort in knowing God doesn't make mistakes. His plans and purpose for our lives isn't always obvious, but please believe that He is constantly ordering our steps and leading us to our ultimate destiny.

Dr. Tony Evans preached a sermon about accepting when it's your time to go. He reminded me that when we have fulfilled our earthly purpose, there is nothing that can be done to save us from death or postpone our deaths. Isaiah 57:1–2 reads, "That the righteous perish, and no one ponders it in his heart; devout men are taken away, and no one understands that the righteous are taken away to be spared from evil. Those who walk uprightly enter into peace; they find rest as they lie in death". Although I believe God equips us with the knowledge and survival skills we need to survive potentially life-threatening situations, I also agree and believe that the only true survival formula is the heavenly Father's will for our lives.

# NEW BEGINNING

Be strong and courageous. Do not be terrified; do not be discouraged, for the Lord your God will be with you wherever you go.

—Joshua 1:9

For several years of my childhood, I lived in one of the most dangerous areas in southwest Houston. The apartment complex where my father, sister, and I resided after my parents divorced was infested with drug activity and gangs. Police cars racing through the streets and helicopters buzzing in the sky were regular occurrences. As a young boy, I was mesmerized by the fast police cars, flashing lights, and blaring sirens. The police officers reminded me of superheroes from my favorite cartoons. They seemed larger than life and powerful. Even the toughest gangsters would cower and retreat when the police arrived. A lot of the kids idolized the drug dealers and thugs, but I felt a strong connection with the police officers, not the criminals. I was impressed by how fearlessly they went after the "bad guys." I spent hours watching police shows such as *Cops* and *City under Siege*. Both shows mimicked my environment. I was intrigued by them because the violence and criminal activity depicted on the

21

screen was exactly what was awaiting me on the other side of my front door. It was during that time in my life that my interest in being a police officer was born. I knew I wanted to be part of the solution, not the problem.

Drugs were at the root of all the crime that plagued my neighborhood. I was exposed to marijuana, crack cocaine, and everything in between before I reached middle school. Every street corner on the block was occupied by drug dealers and gang members, and I routinely witnessed the transactions between the suppliers and addicts. Every time I walked to the convenience store or played outside, I risked being caught in the midst of a drive-by shooting or drug deal gone awry. I was living in the middle of a domestic war zone, and I hated it. The peer pressure and allure of the gangs was constant. We were continuously approached and propositioned to join gangs and sell drugs. At a very young age I knew a life of crime would result in either my death or incarceration. My older brother was constantly in and out of prison. Sports were my outlet and provided a temporary escape from the madness.

Playing sports was my alternative to the drugs and violence. I loved to play basketball, football, and especially baseball. Growing up in the inner city, my friends and I didn't have the luxury of playing on manicured lawns or access to well-kept baseball fields and basketball courts, but that didn't stop us. We were resourceful and used the things scattered throughout the neighborhood to create our own recreation spaces. We didn't have much, but we made the best of what we had. We played football on the concrete and used the apartment dumpster as a backstop for our baseball games. The YMCA—Young Men's Christian Association—also offered us refuge from the violence on the streets. Our parents couldn't afford the membership fees, so we would sneak in to use the facilities. One afternoon, Mr. Bob, one of the staff members at the Westland YMCA, caught us sneaking into the facility. I was certain he was going to kick us out, but instead he sat us down and gave us the surprise of our lives. Mr. Bob waived the membership fees and allowed us to join the YMCA to play sports year-around. I didn't know it at the time, but that was truly a defining moment in my life. Mr. Bob gave us the opportunity to spend our days in a safe, healthy environment instead of roaming the streets and getting into trouble. Focusing on sports kept us out of danger and off the streets.

By the time I reached high school, baseball was my life. I overcame taking off a year to heal from the injuries I sustained in the car accident, and finally my hard work and dedication to the sport paid off. After a successful high school career, I earned a baseball scholarship to Texas Southern University, TSU. I was a starter on the TSU baseball team until I withdrew from college to pursue my dreams of playing professional baseball. I played in the minor leagues from 2001 until 2003, after I decided to hang up the cleats, I returned to TSU and graduated with a Bachelor of Science degree in Criminal Justice. After graduation I decided to pursue a career in the juvenile justice system as a juvenile probation officer. Working with youth, providing them with services to successfully complete their probation, and being a mentor to help them get their lives on the right track was rewarding, but I wasn't content or fulfilled in my job. I needed a change and wanted a career that would allow me to continue to give back to my community in a meaningful way as well as challenge me. As a probation officer there were times I was required to work closely with officers from the Houston Police Department. Working with the police officers reignited the spark within me from my childhood. After careful consideration, I decided it was time to make my childhood dream of being a police officer a reality.

The Houston Police Department application process was very long and tedious. The first step was for me to take the Civil Service Examination. I was confident in my performance on the exam, but disappointed that it took two months before I received an interview with a recruiting officer. After my interview, I completed and submitted the initial application and other required documentation to the recruiting unit. Several weeks later I was assigned a recruiter. My recruiter helped guide me through the rest of the application process, which included a physical training test, drug screening, a psychological evaluation, thorough background and credit checks, vision and hearing screenings, and a polygraph test. Four months after I started the application process, my file was submitted to the Chief of Police for final approval. I was overwhelmed with excitement when I learned my application had been approved. All of the hard work and waiting had finally paid off. In just a few weeks I would be entering Cadet Class 189 at the Houston Police Department Training Academy.

The week before I entered the police academy, I attended a mandatory orientation at police headquarters. The other cadets and I were escorted into a small room at the police station. We listened to presentations by training officers from the academy and from Houston Police Department—HPD—human resources representatives. They gave us a general overview of what to expect at the academy and a list of required supplies. The orientation was informative, but I was most excited about the opportunity to meet and fellowship with the other police trainees. Although they were perfect strangers, I knew that embarking upon this new experience together would bond us for life.

My first day at the academy reminded me of my first day of college. The classroom was set up like those on a typical college campus, with fixed seating arranged in a forward position. There was a small podium at the head of the room, and white dry-erase boards stretched along the width of the front wall. I arrived early on my first day, partly because I was anxious but mostly because I was sure there would be harsh consequences for tardiness. I quietly walked into the room and found my seat. Our seat assignments were in alphabetical order, and my seat was in the last row at the top of the classroom, just like when I was in college. The other cadets and I silently awaited the arrival of our instructors. The room was filled with nervous energy. I was eager to begin this new journey, but a bit on edge because I didn't know what to expect. Were the officers going to storm into the room, yelling and barking orders? Was I going to be called on and asked questions for which I didn't have an answer? My stomach was in knots and my palms were sweating. I was only half an hour early, but it seemed like an eternity before the first instructor arrived. I didn't know whether to stand or stay seated when he entered the room. Fortunately, he told us to keep our seats as he walked to the head of the class.

The first day was very similar to orientation. The majority of the day was spent handling administrative tasks. We filled out several packets of paperwork and received an introduction to the course curriculum. The training officers introduced themselves, explained their expectations, and gave us an outline of the training schedule. They seemed firm but fair. I was pleasantly surprised by the calm atmosphere, but in the back of my mind I knew it was too good to be true. I was certain that this would be the last day we were fortunate enough to begin the day in the comfort of an air-conditioned classroom.

The Houston Police Department Training Academy is an intense six-month program designed to prepare police cadets for successful careers as police officers. It is structured like a military boot camp and focuses on three main components: physical training (PT), academics, and skills. Most of my days at the academy started with at least an hour of physical training. We would usually begin with a morning run or calisthenics. I preferred running because it had an extremely cathartic effect on me. Running allowed me to temporarily forget all the stresses and pressures of the academy. As I ran along the trail, I often thought about the upcoming events of the day. At the end of every run I felt calm and centered. It was a fantastic way to start each day. In addition to cardiovascular exercises, we did a lot of resistance training, such as weight lifting, circuit training, and everyone's favorite, push-ups!

PT was very strenuous and our instructors pushed us to the limits. I didn't always like it, but I knew it was necessary. I had to be in excellent physical shape to meet the physical demands of the job. My physical condition would directly affect my ability to perform daily tasks on the job, and more important, could be the difference between life and death in certain situations on the streets. For this reason, every police cadet was required to pass a five-part physical fitness exam before graduation. The PT exam included a vertical jump test, a push-up test, a three-hundred-meter run, an agility run, and a one-and-a-half-mile run. Each of the exercises on the exam was related to practical tasks police officers typically perform on a daily basis. For example, the one-and-a-half-mile run measures cardiovascular endurance and leg muscle strength. As a police officer I would be placed in emergency situations that required stamina and endurance, such as chasing a fleeing suspect or running to the aid of a citizen in distress. Being physically fit was imperative to my success and survival as a police officer.

I enjoyed learning about different laws that I didn't know even existed, but hated having to rush to class every day. After PT we were allotted only fifteen minutes to shower, dress, and report to the classroom. Sharing showers and a small restroom with more than thirty other men and racing next door every morning was arguably my least favorite thing about the academy. My experience at the academy was about much more than PT and push-ups. In fact, we spent more time on academics than on physical training and skills. The academy is a learning institution focused on educating future law enforcement officials on the law, ethics, and law enforcement rules and regulations. The majority of my coursework was focused on the Texas Penal Code, the Texas Code of Criminal Procedure, and a basic Peace Officer course.

To graduate from the academy, I had to take eight primary exams as well as the Texas Commission on Law Enforcement Officer Standards and Education exam, a mandatory certification exam for all Texas Peace Officers. There were strict standards regarding achieving passing scores on the exams. We were required to maintain a minimum cumulative grade point average of 70 percent. I was passionate about learning about the law and spent hours reading and preparing for class. My discipline and hard work paid off, and I made high marks on all of my exams. However, I was less worried about test scores and more concerned with ensuring I was prepared for life on the streets as a police officer. I knew I needed to be able to recognize and understand the laws I would be responsible for enforcing. Being well versed in the law would allow me to know exactly what I could and couldn't do as a police officer. The instructing officers would usually spend the first half of the class lecturing. The lectures were informative, but I learned the most from the stories they shared with us about real-life incidents they had either experienced or heard about from other officers. Understanding the fundamental principles of the law and procedures of law enforcement as they were described in textbooks gave me the knowledge to pass my exams, but listening to the officers explain the practical application of enforcing those laws and following the procedures helped prepare me for life on the streets as a police officer.

In addition to the PT and academic requirements, we were required to become proficient in several applied skills areas in order to graduate. The skills subjects included firearms training, driver's training, defensive tactics, report writing, emergency medical response care, field problems, and search techniques. Driver's training was my favorite! I loved watching police television shows and movies as a kid, especially the scenes involving action-packed police chases. I was young, naïve, and somewhat disturbingly excited about being in my first high-speed police chase. My adrenaline would start pumping the minute I sat behind the wheel. I felt a rush as I sped around the track and zipped around the curves at dangerous speeds. Sometimes during the training exercises I would envision myself speeding through traffic and chasing a suspect. Driver's training was a kicked-up version of my high school driver's education class. Instead of learning the basics, the driving instructors taught us useful skills such as vehicle handling and weight-transfer techniques for high-speed emergency response and pursuit driving, using the two-way radio while driving and chasing cars, and techniques for avoiding car collisions. We were required to pass each segment of driver's training as well as a comprehensive written exam.

Firearms training was very demanding and my least favorite course at the police academy. The three-week class was taught by some of the most rigid, and at times rude, officers at the academy. I was eager to learn, but their attitudes created a tense, hostile learning environment that made it uncomfortable to ask questions or enjoy the experience. The first week of classroom instruction was dedicated to learning the terminology commonly associated with the various weapons and basic handgun care and safety. We learned how to take apart, clean, lubricate, and clear our weapons if they got jammed during the course of fire. I was looking forward to the second week of training because I thought we were going to immediately begin shooting weapons. I didn't realize how much I had to learn before I would actually get a chance to pull a trigger. The instructors taught us the proper way to hold and grip our pistols, as well as the best method of drawing our weapons from a holster. We practiced drawing from various positions, such as standing, kneeling, and while lying in a prone position.

The field problems were the most challenging part of skills

training. The problems were designed to teach us how to function in dangerous and unpredictable situations. We were presented with problem-based scenarios and went to the different crime scenes with role-playing police officers from the academy. The field problems also gave the officers an opportunity to gauge our progress and identify our individual strengths and weaknesses. As the days progressed, the scenarios became more complex and at times frustrating. One day in particular, I was assigned a partner, and our task was to enter, search, and secure an abandoned warehouse. Shortly after we entered the building, my partner made an error that cost me my pretend life. I was visibly shaken and upset. I knew we were just role-playing, but it had seemed very real. I replayed the incident in my head for hours that night. Every time I closed my eyes, I heard the loud bang from the gun and watched my body sink to the floor. I knew the risks associated with being a police officer, and I thought I'd accepted them before I entered the academy. But I was starting to feel unsure about my decision. It was the first time that I seriously contemplated quitting the police academy. Failing a training exercise was upsetting, but I could always try again the next day. There wouldn't be any second chances once I was working the streets. Being "shot and killed" in the warehouse was a real eye-opener. The reality that there was a high probability that I would be placed in situations where I would have to kill or be killed was staring me in the face. I wanted to protect and serve my community, but I didn't know if I could put my life at risk day after day and night after night. *Should I cut my losses and quit now or should I stay the course and continue to pursue my lifelong dream of being a police officer?* I asked myself. I was confused and didn't know what to do. I meditated and prayed about it. I asked God to order my steps according to His will for my life. Instantly I felt an overwhelming sense of peace and decided to remain in the academy. I knew it was my calling to be a police officer and change lives through police service.

Life at the police academy was demanding and grueling, but it was also one of the best experiences of my life. I forged lifelong friendships with the other cadets, made unforgettable memories, and learned life lessons that proved to be useful in my professional and personal life. I was thrilled the day I graduated from the police academy. After six long months I had become a stronger, smarter, and more disciplined man. I was confident and felt prepared to successfully move forward to the next step in my journey to becoming a police officer. I was eager to see what it was like to be faced with real-world situations rather than those mock scenes from the academy. I looked forward to the field-training program and to learning as much as I could before I got off probation and was out there on my own. I was at the beginning of a prosperous twenty-five-year career. I was finally living the life of my dreams!

# LIFE OF MY DREAMS

Blessed are the peacemakers, for they will be called sons of God.

—Matthew 5:9

The night before going into my first assignment as a rookie officer brought back memories of the night before my first day in high school. I was beyond excited and equally anxious. My uniform was crisp, all of the pins and badges were in their proper places, and my boots were shined to perfection. My mind was consumed with the thoughts of what it would be like to finally get behind the wheel of a police car as an actual officer. As crazy it sounds, I was even looking forward to my first high-speed chase. Just thinking about it gave me an instant adrenaline rush. I was so eager and restless that I managed to get only a few hours of sleep the night before my first day on the job. I was thrilled when my alarm clock sounded the next morning. My big day was finally here, and I was ready!

When I arrived at the police station, I was ordered to report to a room filled with men and women, both young and old and of all ethnic backgrounds. We were all wearing the same uniform, but there was a clear distinction between the enthusiastic rookie officers and the twenty-year veterans who longed for retirement. Many of the more seasoned officers were overweight and out of shape. Their uniforms were old and wrinkled, their boots were dirty and worn out, and their old, scratched, and scarred badges revealed the length of their tenure. As I sat there anxiously waiting to see who my field-training officer would be, I asked myself, *Am I really ready to take on the responsibility of protecting and saving other people's lives?* The answer was a resounding yes, but I really didn't know what to expect. My only point of reference was the stories I'd heard while I was in the police academy. The officers at the academy would often tell us about their personal experiences while working the streets. Some of the stories had happy endings, but the majority of them were tragic and quite shocking. Listening to them talk about rescuing abused and neglected children was extremely difficult, and the stories about finding decomposed bodies covered in maggots and other insects turned my stomach. I was nervous and anxious about the things I was likely to encounter as a police officer. I was entering a violent and unpredictable world, and I knew I had to keep my emotions in check.

I was beginning a prestigious career that would bring about incredible responsibility, challenge, opportunity, and eventually financial stability. But I was still a rookie, which meant I didn't have job security until my probation period ended. The field-training program was very stressful. I was required to read and absorb tons of information as well as implement what I had just learned during that same time period. The learning curve was steep, and each day brought a new opportunity for me to test myself. Fortunately for me, I was able to rise to the task and performed in ways I never thought possible. I was exposed to people and situations I had never dreamed of and became more and more eager to learn as much as I could. My days and nights were consumed with police work. I was on a mission to be the best police officer I could be.

The field-training program consisted of three, three-week

phases: day shift, evening shift, and night shift. During the first phase I worked day shift with a senior officer. We would begin our day at a popular doughnut shop, indulging in fresh, warm pastries and hot coffee. This phase was a lot slower and usually consisted of learning how to type offense reports and fill out paperwork. The second phase was set at a much faster pace and usually involved riding with a younger, more energetic officer. The third phase was intended to give rookie officers an opportunity to experience what it's like to police the streets at night. Incorporating the element of almost total darkness was used to increase awareness and heighten survival skills.

Field training was followed by a two-week evaluation period. It was during this phase that everything I learned in field training was put to the test. It was time for me to prove I had what it took to become a full-fledged police officer. Unfortunately, not everyone successfully completes the evaluation process. Some fail to complete the program, and others realize police work is not the career for them and simply quit. There was no way I was going to leave. I had invested too much time and energy to fail. However, I must admit there was a time during my second phase of training that I wanted to quit. My trainer was a complete jerk. He was rude and arrogant. His negative attitude and comments caused me to doubt my ability. I felt like I wasn't good enough and couldn't do anything right. He was extremely discouraging and negative, and found fault in just about everything I did. He never complimented my performance, and I had no reassurance that I was on the right track. I often left work feeling like a complete failure. I dreaded every day of my second phase and frequently hoped my trainer would not show up for work. Although it wasn't a pleasant experience, I eventually finished phase two and moved on to the final stage of training. In the third phase, I experienced firsthand what it took to become a police officer. I was exposed to every element of crime. I witnessed everything from the aftermath of suicides, fatal car wrecks, violent domestic disputes, and homicides to being shot at by robbery suspects. The third phase of my training ended with a bang. It was on to evaluation, which lasted two weeks. My two weeks of evaluation was on night shift with a senior officer. Everything I had learned and experienced in the three weeks of training had to be put to the test. The evaluator was there to shadow my every move and to make sure I knew how to be a police officer. It was the first time I was able to make decisions on my own. The months of training in the academy and the few weeks of working the streets were finally paying off. I was relaxed and comfortable during the evaluation process and completed the final phase of my training without any issues.

Police work is extremely unpredictable because it is driven by crisis and emergency responses to frequently dangerous situations. I quickly became addicted to the variety and unpredictability of the job and adjusted well to the stresses and challenges it presented. Even after a troublesome day at work, I was so passionate about my job that all I could think about was returning to work the next day. I was twenty-six years old with more power than most people will have in a lifetime. The more I learned, the more confident I became in my ability to perform as a police officer. I ate, slept, and dreamed police work. I arrived early, stayed late, and took advantage of every available hour of overtime. I was assigned to the night shift and worked a ten-hour swing shift with horrible days off, but it didn't matter to me, because I was focused on impressing my coworkers and supervisors with my enthusiasm and heroic acts. I did a lot of foolish things early in my career. Working overtime one evening, I chased a suspect across both north- and southbound lanes of traffic on a freeway during rush hour. I didn't think it was a big deal at the time, but after I had time to process what had actually happened, I realized I had taken an unnecessary, potentially fatal risk of losing my life that day.

Wearing my police uniform did something to me on the

inside. I felt invincible. The moment I put it on, it was as if I was a powerful, brave superhero who could save the world. I looked at every call as a chance to encourage, manipulate, intimidate, or confront others. I was action oriented and authoritative. I always appeared to be in control, on top of things, knowledgeable, and fearless, but that wasn't always the case. I constantly struggled to hide my emotions. As police officers we're taught to keep our composure, particularly when we're confronted with difficult situations, but that isn't always easy. It is difficult to remain poised and professional when a suspect hits, spits on, insults, and humiliates you in front of strangers or coworkers. I have experienced it all, and it never got any easier to handle. It's a bitter pill to swallow, but it's what we signed up for when we took the oath to protect and serve the citizens of our community. Some say you have to lose control in order to gain it. I don't know who came up with something so ridiculous, especially in the midst of absolute chaos.

I remember my first encounter with violence on the job. I was in my third phase of training and pulled a man over for speeding. When I approached the car, it was obvious he was nervous, because he was fumbling around in the car and very fidgety. I asked for his license and insurance and he replied, "Sir, I don't have my license on me, and the car does not have any insurance." I immediately asked him to step out of the car, patted him down for weapons, and placed him in handcuffs. He wasn't under arrest at this point, but I felt it was the best thing to do to ensure my safety. He was visibly nervous, and it was clear he was trying to hide something. I didn't want to take any chances, so I placed him in the back of the patrol car while I ran his information on the computer. It turned out he had only a suspended driver's license, so I couldn't figure out why his behavior was so erratic. While he was in the back of the police car, he started complaining that the handcuffs were too tight and was cutting off his circulation. My trainer opened the door and had him step out so he could loosen the handcuffs. As soon as the suspect stepped out of the police car, he took off running. My trainer started shouting; I immediately looked in the rearview mirror to see what was happening and saw the man running down the street. I jumped out of the car and started to chase him. When we finally caught him, my trainer had one hand on one end of the handcuffs; the guy's other hand was free. I tried to grab his free hand and place it behind his back so we could put him back in the handcuffs. It was then that it became clear that this man really did not want to go to jail and wasn't giving up without a fight. I was doing my best to keep my composure and not allow his antics to frustrate or upset me, but it was nearly impossible after he tried to punch me in the face. The techniques I had learned in the academy were momentarily forgotten, and my survival instincts kicked in. I reached back with my fist balled and landed a solid shot to his chin. He immediately dropped to the ground and appeared to be unconscious. I called the paramedics to the scene to resuscitate and evaluate him before we transported him to jail. That was my first experience of being attacked on the job, but it certainly wouldn't be the last.

In the first two years of my career, I saw more tragedy than the average person sees in a lifetime. I observed the aftermath of fatal car accidents, murders, suicides, and countless other dreadful crimes, and through it all I had to remain calm and composed. Fortunately, I was eventually able to forget some of the incidents I witnessed, but there are two occurrences I'll never forget. The first began when an officer on evening shift was dispatched to a welfare check of a mother and her two children. The family was concerned because it had been days since they had spoken to the mother, and they feared her boyfriend might have done something to hurt her and her children. When the first officer arrived at the scene, he knocked on the door several times, but there was no response. He tried opening the front door, but couldn't get past the burglar bars.

Finally he notified dispatch that he couldn't gain entry to check, so he left and cleared the call as "unfounded," meaning "unable to be located." As the hours passed, the mother's family became increasingly worried that something was wrong, because she had never gone so many hours without contacting relatives or friends. Additionally, she hadn't showed up for work that day, and the kids missed school. They knew something wasn't right and contacted police a second time to have an officer meet them at her house. When the police arrived, one of the family members decided to break one of the bedroom windows so she could go in to see if anyone was inside. She crawled inside the broken window and discovered the bodies of the mother and her two daughters. All three had been brutally attacked and murdered.

When I arrived at the scene, the apartment complex was surrounded by reporters and cameramen from every news station in the city. The family members of the victims were huddled together, crying and grieving the losses of their loved ones. I could feel the grief and despair in the air as everyone stood around looking for answers. This was the first time I felt helpless and useless, and I could tell by the looks on the other officers' faces that I wasn't alone. This was by far the worst thing that I'd ever seen. I did my best, but it was impossible to hide my emotions. Nothing I had learned in the police academy or in my on-the-job training had prepared me to deal with what I had just witnessed. I walked out of that apartment shaking my head in sadness and confusion. Who would commit such a terrible crime? I was overcome with emotion, but I knew I had to stay focused and keep my personal feelings in check. I took a moment to gather my thoughts and reminded myself that there was nothing I could've done to save that family. I had to push through and do my job.

The family members of the victims were adamant that the mother's boyfriend was responsible for the murders. They told us he was an ex-convict who had recently been released on parole after serving ten years in prison for aggravated robbery. We were gathering as much information from the family as possible so we could begin searching for the boyfriend. He was our primary suspect. Needless to say, we were all shocked when he casually walked up to the scene of the crime where he had killed his girlfriend and her two daughters as if nothing had happened. As soon as he appeared, one of the family members shouted, "There he is!" In that moment, it seemed like every officer on the scene ran full speed ahead toward him to make sure he was apprehended as quickly and safely as possible. Much to our surprise, he didn't try to run away or struggle. He surrendered with ease. He had just crawled out of a manhole, and his hands and clothes were covered in mud and blood. He was expressionless and didn't seem to have any remorse for taking three innocent lives. I wanted to kill him for what he had done, but I knew I couldn't let this one incident get the best of me. The night was still young, and although I had just witnessed an unspeakable tragedy, I still had eight hours remaining on my shift. Again, I had to find the strength to push through and do my job.

The next day I decided to take a few days off from work to ease my mind and get away from the harsh realities of the job. I was only two years into my career and had already seen dozens of bodies of murder victims and other violent crimes. It was starting to take a toll on me. The time off was exactly what I needed. I returned to work refreshed and with a renewed sense of purpose. I was actually able to enjoy my job again. The nature of the work didn't change; my perspective did. I made a conscious decision to focus on the lives I was saving and not dwell on the tragedies I couldn't prevent. Unfortunately, it took only one call to change everything.

When I started my shift on December 27, 2007, it seemed like just another ordinary day on the job. It was cold and rainy, and there weren't many people out on the streets. The number of calls for service was down, and I was hopeful it would be a relatively peaceful night. A few hours into my shift I was dispatched to a robbery in progress. The details of the call were sketchy. I wasn't exactly sure what I would actually find when I arrived, because a major car accident was reported at the same location and the dispatcher notified me that shots had been fired. Several thoughts were racing through my mind as I was driving to the scene: *What if I have to shoot someone? What if I kill someone? What if I get shot? What if someone kills me?* I was afraid and expecting the worst. This wasn't like being at the police academy. This was a real-life situation with potentially deadly consequences.

My heart was racing and my adrenaline was pumping as I pulled into the convenience-store parking lot. I was advised by dispatch that two suspects were involved in the attempted robbery of the store. I quickly exited my police vehicle and entered the store to speak with the clerk. He informed me he had shot at the suspects and they both left the store immediately. One of the suspects fled into a nearby apartment complex, and the other was killed after crashing into a parked eighteen-wheeler around the corner from the store. In the midst of all the chaos, I realized that had I arrived just a few seconds earlier, I would have been in the middle of a deadly confrontation.

The other officers on the scene were tending to the store clerk, who was visibly shaken up. They were doing their best to calm him down and get his account of what had taken place. I decided to walk around the corner to investigate the car accident. The suspect was still inside his truck, which was smashed up against the semi. The dome lights were on and you could clearly see inside. I cautiously approached the suspect's vehicle, even though I was certain he was dead. I couldn't afford to be caught off guard by any surprises. I noticed that he had sustained two gunshot wounds, one to the right side of his chest and one right below near his stomach. I could see the two small holes in his sweat shirt where the bullets penetrated. Rigor mortis had already set in. His right hand was clenched in a fist, still holding tight to the money he had stolen during the robbery. I didn't immediately recognize him, but something about him was vaguely familiar. I thought maybe I had arrested him in the past. It wasn't until I inspected the body more closely that I noticed a burn on the man's left hand. I paused briefly and took a closer look at his face. I couldn't believe my eyes. The "suspect" was my older brother, Willie Roy. Words can't adequately convey my shock, horror, and embarrassment. I froze, my knees buckled, and I fell to the ground. I completely lost control of my emotions and could no longer function as a police officer.

Everything changed the moment I saw my brother's face. What started out as an unknown robbery call ended up becoming a personal tragedy. I was no longer just a police officer responding to a call; I was a younger brother. The dead person inside the truck wasn't a suspect; he was my big brother. And the store clerk went from being the victim of a crime to the man who had just shot and killed my brother. My world was turned upside down in an instant. I felt completely helpless. I gathered my emotions as best as I could, took one last look at Willie's body, and returned to the store to explain the situation to the other officers. After letting my supervisors know that the suspect inside the truck was my brother, I had to leave the scene immediately per department policy. As I drove away, questions started racing through my mind: How was I going to explain to my dad that Willie was dead? Was it really necessary for the store clerk to shoot him? Did I still want to be a police officer after seeing my brother killed?

My sister and father met me at the police station so I could give them the news. My dad was overwhelmed, and broke down inside his truck in the station's parking lot. After I received instructions on what I had to do, we left the police station and went home. We spent the night wondering what had gone wrong and what would drive my brother to do such a thing. Watching my father grieve for his son was extremely difficult. The sorrow in his eyes was unbearable. He was heartbroken, and there wasn't anything I could do to fix it. I felt powerless. My emotions were all over the place. I was experiencing grief, anger, guilt, and uncertainty. I was sad about the loss of my brother and angry with the store clerk for shooting him. I couldn't help but wonder if he would still be alive if I had made it to the scene sooner, or whether I would have been the one to take his life. And for the first time in my career, I questioned my desire to be a police officer. I remember taking off my police uniform and staring at it. The same uniform that I had proudly worn didn't seem to mean as much anymore and looked like nothing more than a shirt and pair of pants. It was then that I knew I was forever changed.

I took some time off from work to grieve with my family and process my emotions. I spent the first few hours after I returned home from the police station in a state of shock. I always knew my brother's drug addiction would result in another stint in prison or death, but I couldn't wrap my mind around the undeniable fact that he was actually dead. We weren't the closest brothers in the world, but in spite of his shortcomings and issues, I loved him dearly and knew he loved me. He was my big brother, and losing him in such a violent manner for such a senseless reason took a tremendous toll on me. I couldn't sleep, because every time I dozed off, I would have nightmares about the night he was killed. I eventually accepted that there wasn't anything I could've done to save him the day he died, but I wondered if I could've prevented the entire incident if I had done more to help him get treatment for his addiction.

My brother had spent the last several years of his life battling an addiction to alcohol and crack cocaine. All of his criminal activity and poor choices stemmed from his drug addiction. He needed to support his habit and was willing to do the unthinkable to get money for drugs. Willie had reached out to me shortly before he died. He confided that he was having urges to do drugs and was afraid he was on the verge of another relapse. I told him to be strong and fight the cravings. I reminded him that he needed to stay clean and sober for himself so that he could be a better father and husband. He took my advice and checked himself into a rehabilitation facility. Everyone was hopeful this time would be different, but two weeks later, he checked himself out and relapsed. Eventually he lost his job and resorted to robbing stores to get money to buy crack.

The conversation between my brother and me replayed in my head for months. I felt guilty that I hadn't been more sensitive to his desperate cries for help. I didn't blow him off, but I felt like I hadn't given him the time, attention, and assistance he needed. He was sick and fighting a disease, and I had callously assumed he could just resist the temptation if he tried hard enough. My brother needed professional help to overcome his addiction, not a pep talk. He wasn't a bad person. He was an addict who made poor choices that resulted in his untimely death, but his death was not in vain.

It took several years for me to recognize it, but now I understand God used Willie's demise to teach me a costly lesson in unconditional love and compassion to prepare me for my destiny. I am dedicated to sharing God's word with all of His children. I no longer live in the space that allowed me to judge others and value their sins greater than my own. I am a more compassionate, empathetic Christian. It is my sincere hope and prayer that my message will empower men and women like Willie and help them realize that with God's help, they can take their lives from zero to a hundred.

Before returning to work, I was ordered to see a psychiatrist. Discussing what had happened and sharing my thoughts was helpful, but it didn't change how I felt. The night my brother was killed, I had a mental shift. My attitude changed from that of a dedicated public servant to that of an angry, vengeful person with a badge. After a couple of weeks of desk duty, I started patrolling the streets again. My enthusiasm and dedication for police work was replaced with pessimism and vengeance. I didn't care about protecting and serving the community any more. My mission was to avenge my brother's death. I took every robbery call that was dispatched in the area in hopes of confronting an armed robber face-to-face. My intention was to take another person's life so that their family could experience the same pain I was feeling. None of my coworkers knew the emotional turmoil I felt on the inside. I was trapped between two worlds. On the outside I appeared to be this brave, energetic, and competent cop, but I was actually a vindictive, resentful, and monstrous person motivated by anger and revenge.

It didn't take long before my patrol supervisors started to wonder why I was so adamant about taking all the robbery calls. My behavior caused my supervisors to be concerned and suspicious. My sergeants knew that something was terribly wrong and had me report back to the station for a meeting. I told them the reason for my eager response to robbery calls and the way I was feeling about my brother's death. They understood my dilemma and felt it would be best if I was back off the streets until I fully mourned the loss of my brother and dealt with my emotions. After an additional three weeks off and a few more therapy sessions, I still found myself experiencing great ambivalence about returning to the streets. My confidence was at an all-time low, and I often questioned whether I should continue as a cop or seek a new profession. My greatest fear was encountering a real robbery where I would be forced to pull the trigger. I thought about how I would be viewed by my peers and supervisors. Would they look at me as protecting and serving or as nothing more than a civilian with a badge whose sole purpose was to avenge his brother's death?

I began second-guessing myself all the time. I was afraid that the probability of being seriously injured on the job was greater because of my indecisiveness.

The take-charge cop I used to be had been erased by my own skepticism. I was caught between a rock and a hard place. I had to make some tough decisions. I could take more time off and seek additional counseling; continue to patrol the streets, which were filled with danger and bad memories; or cut my losses and walk away from the prestigious career I had worked so hard to attain. Although it took some time to accept what had happened, I decided to stay, because I felt like being a police officer was my calling. I had no idea what the days ahead would bring, but I was determined to crawl out of this dark hole of depression and anger. I still enjoyed some aspects of my job, but the passion I had once had started to dissipate, and the thrill was gone. Fantasies about the job had been replaced with a more realistic acceptance of working long hours for low pay, tons of paperwork, the influence of politics, and flaws in our judicial system.

Being exposed to so much negativity and violence changed my view of the world, especially my trust and admiration for others. I saw the worst in people's behavior on a daily basis. It took only a few disappointments before I built a wall of cynicism to protect myself. I didn't trust anyone, not even my closest family members or friends. I had tunnel vision, and I was comfortable associating only with other cops. I carried my gun everywhere, even the few times I attended church. I viewed everyone as a criminal and a potential threat. Few people were worthy of my time. I started to focus less on trying to advance in the department and more on accumulating financial wealth and material possessions.

I would work sixteen-hour shifts four times a week. I was a workaholic focused on making as much money as possible. The drive to want more was based on my own misconceptions that having more would make me feel happier, more important, and more secure. How ignorant was I? My life was defined and driven by money and material things. Eventually I realized that the high I felt from the money and the things was fleeting, and was never enough. It was a vicious cycle. I would buy new things, become bored with them, focus on the things I didn't have, and work longer hours to buy more things. I didn't understand that my value was not determined by my worldly possessions, but was instead determined by my relationships with God, my family, and how I treated other people. I had sold my soul to the devil for money. I sacrificed everything that was truly important to me so I could work seven days and more than eighty hours a week. I was a slave to money. Money was my drug of choice. It was intoxicating and began to rule my life. Possessions and money became a substitute for my real identity. The strong Christian man I thought I had become was a figment of my imagination. I thought I was living the life of my dreams. I thought I was in control, but had no idea that what would occur next would change my life forever.

# 6 END OF WATCH

> He rescued me from my powerful enemy, from my foes, who were too strong for me. They confronted me in the day of my disaster, but the Lord was my support. He brought me out into a spacious place; he rescued me because he delighted in me.
>
> —Psalm 18:17–19

**M**y partner, Gerald, and I were looking forward to the end of another long shift so we could get home to our families. One of the advantages of working the night shift was that my girlfriend and our seven month old son, Jadon, were usually awake and waiting to greet me when I arrived home from work. The anticipation of seeing my son's smiling face was enough to help me push through the long hours. On this particular night, Gerald and I were patrolling one of Houston's high drug-traffic areas and were on heightened alert for any suspicious activity. At approximately 3:30 a.m., we attempted to stop a man for failure to use a signal while making a left turn. It was our last traffic stop of the night, and nothing seemed out of the ordinary. I pulled behind the vehicle and initiated my lights and sirens. When the car pulled over, I started to put my police car in park. Before I could finish shifting the gear, the vehicle sped off. I instinctively stepped on the gas and raced after the car. Everything was happening so fast that I didn't have time to think; all I could do was react. In the blink of an eye, we went from making a routine traffic stop to being in the midst of a high-speed chase. Seconds later, we had both reached speeds of well over a hundred miles per hour. The suspect had no regard for the other drivers and pedestrians on the street. He ignored every traffic signal and stop sign we encountered. He was determined to get away, and he didn't care whom he hurt or killed in the process.

My partner immediately notified dispatch that we had a suspect refusing to stop. He continued to update her on our location as I focused every bit of energy I had on keeping up with the suspect's vehicle. We flew through several red lights before turning onto a street that was completely dark. A voice suddenly whispered in my ear and told me to put my seat belt on, so I did. There weren't any streetlights to help guide me, and the high beams from my headlights offered little assistance. I was doing my best to navigate the dark, rural road, but the flashing red lights and gigantic dust clouds from the suspect's vehicle further impaired my visibility. The suspect continued to increase his speed, and so did I. I was driving over a hundred miles an hour in unfamiliar territory and could barely see what was in front of me. I certainly didn't realize I was quickly approaching "Dead Man's Curve." Suddenly, the red taillights from the vehicle in front of us vanished. It was pitch black, and we were headed toward the S-curve at the end of the two-lane road. I slammed on my brakes to avoid crashing into the ditch, but it was too late. I lost control of the car. I lost my grip on the steering wheel and heard Gerald yell, "Here we go!" The police car flipped over several times before finally landing in the ditch, which was filled with debris from countless other accidents that had ended in the same spot.

When the car finally came to rest in the ditch, I knew I was in trouble. I tried to remain calm, but I was terrified. I didn't have enough energy to yell over the noise of the siren, so in a calm, still voice I called my partner's name and hoped he would hear me. A few seconds later, Gerald reached over and turned off the siren. Fortunately he had only a couple of bruises and somehow managed to force his way out of the car. He climbed out of the ditch and alerted dispatch about the accident. He told them I was trapped in the car and needed immediate medical attention. I knew my injuries were severe because I couldn't move, nor could I feel my arms, legs, fingers, or toes. My left arm was dislocated and dangled outside the driver's-side door.

I was in shock and confused. I didn't understand how I could be paralyzed yet in excruciating pain. The roof of the patrol car had collapsed around me and covered my right shoulder. From the chest down, my body hung outside the vehicle, but I was still pinned in the driver's seat. In spite of the inability to move, I was most concerned about the damage to my head. Every time the car flipped, it felt like I was diving head first into an empty concrete pool. The cut on my head stretched from one ear to the other and was so deep that the back of my scalp was sagging downward and the top of my skull was exposed. I asked Gerald how my head looked. He quickly responded, "Not bad," but I knew he was lying. My head was burning, and blood was flowing from every part of my body like water from a garden hose. It was leaking uncontrollably into my eyes, ears, and mouth, and my uniform was saturated. I wanted to wipe it away, but no matter how hard I tried, I couldn't move my arms or hands.

I sat motionlessly in the remains of the patrol car, feeling like I was drowning in my own blood. I was in utter disbelief that my final moments on Earth were going to be spent paralyzed, trapped in a police car. I was in so much pain and the damage to my body was so extensive that I didn't think I could survive. When my partner returned to my side, I told him I knew I was going to die and asked him to tell my son how much I loved him. He did his best to assure me I was going to be okay. He reminded me of how I had survived another car accident seventeen years earlier, but I told him this time was different. He continued to encourage me to fight to stay alive for myself and my son, but as I choked on my own blood, I was sure I was going to die. I closed my eyes and instinctively started to pray aloud. I prayed a prayer of salvation and asked God to forgive me of my sins. As I was praying, I started to think about my seven-month-old son, Jadon, and saw an image of his face. In that moment I decided I couldn't give up. I cried out to the Lord and begged Him to save my life.

Officer Diego Morelli had been following us during the chase and was the first to come to our aid. He leaped into the ditch and did his best to keep me alive until the firemen and paramedics arrived. I remember whispering to him, "I'm about to die" and asking him to lift my head because I couldn't breathe. Years later my partner confided in me that in spite of his efforts to motivate me to live that night, he actually saw himself speaking at my funeral after I told Morelli I was having trouble breathing. As I drifted in and out of consciousness, I started to doubt whether or not I was going to make it. Finally, I heard the faint sounds of the sirens approaching. When the rescue crew arrived on the scene, they didn't attempt to move my body or try to get me out immediately. Firefighter Cornelius Burton relieved Officer Morelli and took over the task of holding my neck. He immediately started talking and tried to keep me as calm and stable as possible. I was gasping for air and frantically telling him to make sure he continued to support my neck. I could feel my body going into shock, and as each second passed, the pain was becoming more and more unbearable.

After the entire rescue team arrived, they started strategizing about how to extract me from the wreckage. They had to make sure my head and neck were stable and secure before they could attempt to remove me from the car. The biggest obstacle was that the car was nearly upside down in the ditch and that the ground surrounding the ditch was extremely uneven. Additionally, they had to devise a plan to untangle the car door from around my neck without causing further injury to my spine. Captain Valerie Seymour determined that the best course of action was to have a crew who worked with the Jaws of Life—an extrication device— cut me out of the car. Before they started to cut the door off the car, they placed a white sheet over my head to protect my open wounds from the debris. As soon as they placed the sheet over my head, I had a flashback of the night of the accident in 1994. I thought they had given up on me and thought I was dead. I started to panic and struggled to do whatever I could to let them know I was alive. Fireman Burton pulled the sheet back and explained why it was necessary to cover my face. I calmed down and braced myself for the extraction. I wanted to be freed from the car, but I was scared I would die in the process.

I was conscious as they worked frantically yet carefully to remove my limp and nearly lifeless body from the car. It took several people to hoist me out of the ditch and carry me to the stretcher. By this time, scores of police officers and firefighters were on the scene. I heard some of them shouting words of encouragement as they rolled me toward the ambulance. However, I also heard someone say, "It doesn't look good; he might not make it." I knew my injuries were serious, but hearing someone speak those words was terrifying. Once again, the negative thoughts of death started to fill my mind. I told Gerald to call my father immediately. I needed my family to get to the hospital as soon as possible. I was in so much pain and so frightened by my colleague's dreadful prediction that I didn't know if I would survive the ride to the emergency room.

On the ride to the hospital, I periodically tried to move my arms and legs, but I couldn't. I asked the paramedics if I was paralyzed. They said it was too early to tell because my body was still in shock, but I didn't believe them. I thought to myself, *If I can't feel anything, then I must be paralyzed.* My eyes were literally filled with blood, sweat, and tears. I asked one of the paramedics to wipe them for me, but he said he couldn't. I felt completely helpless. All I could do was lie on the stretcher and pray that the pain would magically disappear.

The drive to the ER was the longest and most painful trip of my life. I was relieved when the ambulance came to a screeching halt and the back doors swung open. The paramedics quickly lifted me out of the back of the wagon and rushed me inside the ER. The corridor leading to the emergency room was filled with police officers. More than a dozen police cars had escorted the ambulance to Memorial Hermann Hospital, and officers from all over the city rushed to the hospital to offer their support to my family and me. I was deeply touched as I passed the officers lined up along the walkway and hallways. Some offered words of encouragement, and others simply reached out and touched my bloodied and battered body as the gurney raced past them. I was amazed at the outpouring of love and concern and was proud to be part of such a loyal, remarkable group of men and women. Shortly before I went into surgery, I received visits from Mayor Annise Parker and Police Chief Charles McClelland. I was astounded that they had taken time from their busy schedules to come to the hospital, before dawn, to meet with me, a regular police officer who was just doing his job. They were both extremely concerned about my well-being and offered kind words of support and encouragement. The meetings were brief but meaningful. I was fighting for my life, and it meant the world to me to know the police department and the city of Houston were fighting with me.

*Déjà vu,* the French term that literally means "already seen," perfectly describes how I felt as the paramedics pushed me through the swinging emergency room doors of Memorial

Hermann Hospital. There was an uncomfortable familiarity. My mind raced back and forth between the present and the past. The sights and sounds of the paramedics, doctors, and nurses working frantically to save my life unlocked hidden memories from my previous visit to the ER. Seventeen years earlier, I had been in an eerily similar situation after being in a major automobile accident with a drunk driver. I'd narrowly escaped death that time, but I wasn't sure if I'd be so fortunate again. I was in an incredible amount of pain and couldn't catch my breath. As I gasped for air, I was convinced that every breath I took would be my last.

The trauma team immediately started assessing my injuries. Doctors and nurses were coming at me at lightning speed from every direction. The attending physicians didn't have the luxury of time. Every second was crucial and had the power to determine whether I lived or died. The nurses removed my gun belt and secured it before cutting off my bloody uniform. A reflex hammer stroked against the bottom of my feet to test for any sensation. There was none! It reminded me of a scene from a movie. The only reaction I could show were the tears that rolled down my face onto the stretcher. The doctors immediately started ordering tests and taking computed tomography scans, also known as CT or CAT scans, of my neck and skull. The images showed cervical spinal fractures, ranging from C3 to C7 of my cervical spine (neck) and compression fractures in my thoracic spine stretching from T1 to T6. In layman's terms, my neck and upper back were broken. I had a severe laceration across the top of my head that was so deep and wide, it had to be held together by one of the firefighters who rescued me; a fractured sternum; and numerous broken ribs.

In addition to the physical injuries, an MRI of my head revealed a cerebral infarction, commonly known as a stroke. The stroke was the result of a disturbance in the blood vessels responsible for supplying blood to my brain and was likely caused by the trauma to my head. Having a stroke exacerbated my situation exponentially. Compounding the effects of a stroke and a spinal cord injury is like mixing fire with gasoline. The surgeons quickly reviewed the test results, prioritized my injuries, and developed a surgical schedule. Because of the severity of the cervical fractures I sustained, Dr. Karl Schmitt, the lead neurologist on my case, determined they would tackle my spinal cord injury first, followed by a procedure to repair the scalp wound. Everything was moving so rapidly, I didn't have time to process what was happening. I was terrified and hoped my parents would get to the hospital soon. I was grateful for the support from my fellow officers, but I needed the security and reassurance that only a parent could provide.

I was relieved when my mom and dad showed up, but the relief didn't last long. I knew I was in bad shape, but the horrified looks on their faces indicated that things were worse than I thought. They did their best to stay strong for me, but it was painfully obvious they were on the brink of breaking down. Before they wheeled me into surgery, I asked my mother, "Mom, is my head okay?" She could hardly respond as she struggled to keep her composure and searched for the right words. She told me it didn't look too bad and that I was going to be okay, but her eyes told a completely different story. We said our goodbyes, and I closed my eyes as the gurney carrying my broken body burst through the doors of the operating room.

*Rescue team carefully extracting Jason from police car*

*Daytime view of police car after crash*

*Side view of police car after crash*

*A view of white sheet that was placed over Jason's head during extraction*

*View of driver side damage where Jason was sitting*

# 7 BROKEN

> Dear friends, do not be surprised at the painful trial
> you are suffering, as though something strange
> were happening to you. But rejoice that you
> participate in the sufferings of Christ, so that you
> may be overjoyed when his glory is revealed.
>
> —1 Peter 4:12–13

The operating room was just as busy as the ER. When the doors opened, I saw several doctors and nurses scrambling around the room. Some were turning on monitors and arranging surgical instruments, and others were looking at what I assumed to be my medical charts and talking amongst themselves. A group of nurses and assistants carefully lifted me off the stretcher and gently placed me on the operating table, and within seconds they were prepping me for surgery. A breathing tube was inserted down my throat so I could breathe with the assistance of a ventilator. I wasn't looking forward to having surgery, but the idea of being completely sedated for several hours was quite appealing. I was on board with anything that would relieve the pain. Dr. Schmitt, the lead neurosurgeon, offered a few words of encouragement before the anesthesiologist started administering the drugs, but I was still petrified. I honestly didn't think I would survive the surgery because I was in so much pain and felt so weak. I needed a miracle.

I closed my eyes and prayed like my life depended on it, because it did! I asked God to come into the operating room and perform a miracle through the doctors and nurses. I asked Him to equip them with the knowledge; skills, strength, and stamina they needed to save my life and put my body back together. I prayed for comfort and peace for my friends and family as they nervously awaited the outcome of my surgery. And finally I said a special prayer for my son, Jadon. I surrendered him to the Lord and asked God to keep and guide him all the days of his life. My life was hanging in the balance. I didn't know if I would live to continue to be a father to my son, and I needed to make sure Jadon was covered by the almighty Father. After I said my prayers and relinquished the entire situation to God, the fear and anxiety ceased.

Addressing my spinal cord injury was the first and most urgent priority. The compression fractures along my neck and back were applying too much pressure to my spinal cord, thereby causing the paralysis. The surgeons performed an anterior cervical decompression and stabilization procedure to relieve the pressure and stabilize my neck. I was on my back for the duration of the surgery. A transverse (horizontal) incision was made toward the bottom of my neck so the surgeons could expose the front of my cervical spine and remove the tissue and bone fragments causing the pressure. The goal was to restore as much neurological function as possible, but only time would tell how well it would work, if at all. The surgery lasted approximately seven hours and was a test of endurance for me and the surgical team. I still needed another operation to repair the broken bones in my neck and back, but Dr. Schmitt decided it would be best to give me a day to rest before moving forward with the second spinal procedure.

Shortly after the first surgery was complete, a team of plastic surgeons, led by Dr. Donald Parks, performed a second procedure to repair my scalp wound. I had a horizontal laceration, measuring between twelve and fourteen centimeters, across the top of my head. It was so extensive and deep that it ripped through the surface covering my skull and left a large portion of it exposed. Fortunately, it was still intact. The wound was grossly contaminated with soil, grass, and windshield fragments. It had to be extensively irrigated with saline and an antibiotic solution to ensure all of the debris was removed before it was closed. After the wound was thoroughly decontaminated, they used more than half a foot of non-absorbable, nylon sutures to sew it back together. The surgery was successful, and there were no complications. The spinal decompression and scalp repair combined took approximately twelve hours, further fatiguing my already weary body.

Dr. Schmitt met with my family to update them on my condition. They were elated to learn I had made it through both procedures without any complications. There was a collective sigh of relief in the waiting room when they received the good news, but there was one question at the forefront of everyone's mind: "Will Jason ever walk again?" Dr. Schmitt explained that it was too soon to make any predictions about my long-term prognosis; he said it would be eighteen months before he had an answer to that question.

Two days later it was time for my third and final surgery, a posterior cervical fusion (PCF). PCF is the medical term used to describe the process of surgically mending multiple cervical spine bones together, using an incision on the back of the neck. An eight-inch vertical incision was made down the middle of my neck. A bone graft was placed along the sides of the spine bones, and metal plates, screws, and titanium rods were inserted to align and further stabilize it. Over time the bone grafts would fuse the bones back together. The surgery went as planned without any complications, and I returned to ICU in serious but stable condition to recover. I was now the real-life Robocop.

I was heavily medicated and spent most of my first few days in the intensive care unit drifting in and out of consciousness. I was connected to more tubes, lines, and wires than I could count, and my bed was surrounded by several monitors and IV stands. My feet were placed in compression boots, or as I call them "space boots," to keep them upright, and I had to wear a Miami J collar twenty-four hours a day. The "collar" was a hard plastic neck brace designed to keep my neck straight and stabilized. I couldn't talk, eat, or swallow because of the breathing tube down my throat, so I was fed through a nasogastric, or NG, tube. The tube was inserted down my nostril into my esophagus and pushed down into my stomach. A week after my initial surgery, an inferior vena cava filter was inserted into my femoral vein, on the inside of my upper thigh. Paralysis increases the risk of developing blood clots. The filter helped prevent potentially life-threatening blood clots from forming and traveling to my lungs. I hated having so many cords and gadgets attached to every part of my body. I looked and felt like a life-sized science experiment.

Losing the ability to move was devastating, but the loss of privacy and independence was by far the most humiliating part of being paralyzed. Losing control of my ability to handle my personal hygiene and bathroom needs was embarrassing and disgusting. I felt dirty and was sure I smelled bad. I hadn't been able to bathe since I'd arrived at the hospital two weeks earlier. The breathing tube from the ventilator made it impossible to brush my teeth, and my once clean-shaven face was covered with a long, itchy beard. I couldn't get up to go to the restroom since I was confined to my hospital bed, so I had to use a condom catheter to drain and collect my urine. I don't know if the catheter was defective or if it wasn't attached properly, but it fell off repeatedly and left me soaked in urine. And if that wasn't degrading enough, there were also times I was forced to lie in my own waste until one of the nurses showed up to change me. One time in particular the nurse on duty decided to wait until I had a second bowel movement before he would wash me off and change my gown and bed pad. I was outraged when he said he'd come back after I "went again." The shock quickly turned to shame as I lay in my own filth. There were so many things I wanted to say and do to the nurse, but all I could do was lie there and weep quietly. Days earlier I had been a self-sufficient thirty-two-year-old man, and now I had been reduced to soiling myself like an infant. I was a hostage in my own body and totally helpless. It was a miserable, shameful existence.

I was blessed to have such an awesome support system. The only bright spot in my otherwise dreadful life was the support I received from family and friends. From the moment I arrived at the emergency room, they rallied around me, offering prayers, words of encouragement, and unconditional love. I was amazed at how quickly everyone gathered at the hospital the morning of my accident. They could've easily called or texted to express their concern, but instead they chose to be present and never left me alone. My extended family at the Houston Police Department was also a great source of support. They were there for me from day one of my accident and remained by my side throughout my entire stay at Memorial Hermann and beyond. I received so many visitors that the other patients and their families complained to the hospital administrators because the halls were filled with police officers night and day. Two officers were posted at my hospital room door around the clock for my support and to make sure there weren't any unwelcomed visitors, and my lieutenant, Steve Casko, visited me every day I was in the hospital. As the days passed, the excessive number of visitors never diminished. No matter what time of day or night I opened my eyes; there was a familiar face in my room, and sometimes even an unfamiliar one. My father rarely left my bedside. He sacrificed his own health to personally make sure I was receiving the best possible care. His dedication to me and to my recovery was unparalleled. The love, support, and attention from my family, friends, and colleagues provided comfort the pain medication could not.

The only thing missing was my son. He was too young to visit me in the intensive care unit, and part of me didn't want him to see me in such bad shape. I desperately wanted to see his face and feel his tiny arms around my neck. I missed him so much, it literally made me sick. I was in my darkest hour, and he was my motivation to live. I wanted to hold him, but I couldn't. Instead I held tightly to the happy memories from the first seven months of his life. I thought about how his eyes lit up when I walked through the door and picked him up. I pictured the big grin on his face when I tossed him in the air and blew on his tummy. Unfortunately, those memories were bittersweet. They brought me joy in my time of sorrow, but pain as I wondered if I'd ever be able to be a "normal" dad again.

The beginning of my third week in ICU was marginally better than the previous weeks. I was still in an incredible amount of pain, but I'd reached a couple of milestones that made life a little better. Moments of happiness were virtually nonexistent while I was in the intensive care unit; however, I was legitimately delighted the day the ice pad was removed from my bed. Lying on top of a freezing pad of ice twenty-four hours a day felt like cruel and unusual punishment. Each time one of the nurses took my temperature, I hoped the thermometer reading would be normal, but I was continuously disappointed. After two long weeks of torture, my fever finally broke and my body temperature went back to normal. I was relieved when they took the ice pad away. I was still in pain, but the warmth of the bed sheet was a major improvement over the subzero temperatures I had been forced to endure.

It was an exciting day when the doctors determined I was strong enough to breathe without the assistance of the ventilator. The breathing tube was a painful nuisance and had rendered me completely mute for more than two weeks. I was grateful to the ventilator for sustaining me when I was too weak to breathe on my own, but I couldn't wait to be rid of the tube down my throat. The removal of the breathing tube from my airway was exceedingly painful. I felt like I was suffocating and choking to death as the tube carefully made its way up my esophagus. It wasn't until it was completely out that I felt some relief. My lips were chapped, my throat was dry and sore, and swallowing was especially painful. I had so much to say that I didn't know where to begin. It took me several minutes to build up the courage to try to speak, but when I did, I didn't recognize the sound coming out of my mouth. My voice was hoarse, and I could barely speak above a whisper, but I was satisfied to be able to talk again. The ability to communicate was just one of many precious gifts I'd previously taken for granted.

There are no words to accurately describe the intensity of the chronic pain I experienced every second of every day in the ICU. How could I be paralyzed yet in such excruciating pain? It didn't make any sense. My doctors explained that I was suffering from neuropathic pain caused by the damage to my nerves. My body felt like it was on fire! The lightest touch felt like thousands of pins and needles piercing through my skin. If this bore any resemblance to what hell feels like, then Lord, please spare my soul. I tried to escape the pain by going to sleep, but the freezing ice pad between my back and the bed sheet made it impossible for me to get any rest. Shortly after I arrived in the ICU, my temperature spiked. In an effort to reduce the fever, I had to lie on a large, rectangular ice pad twenty-four hours a day. I wanted to pull the pad from under my body, but I couldn't move. I tried to will my hands and arms to work, but they refused to comply. It was torture!

The nurses tried giving me sleeping pills and other pain medications, but nothing helped. I cried and complained, but nobody would listen. The nurses' solution for every issue was to pump me full of painkillers, but none of them touched the pain or helped me sleep. I was in a perpetual state of agony and deliriously fatigued. After trying multiple combinations of different pain medications, the doctors prescribed large doses of morphine. The morphine provided a temporary reprieve from the pain, but the side effects greatly outweighed its benefits. I became extremely paranoid and started hallucinating almost immediately. I heard voices and saw odd patterns and objects on the walls. The hallucinations were so real; I couldn't decipher reality from my imagination. I felt like I was losing my mind. One afternoon a group of Native Americans walked through the door and stopped at the foot of my hospital bed. They were laughing and talking loudly amongst themselves. I looked at my father, who was sitting on a couch across from my bed, waiting for him to acknowledge the presence of these strangers who had just invaded my room, but he never looked up. I started shouting, "What are you doing in here?" and "Get out before I call security!" My dad asked me whom I was talking to as he scanned the room with a confused expression on his face. I couldn't understand why he was pretending not to see the men standing less than ten feet away from him. I continued to yell at them as my father tried to assure me we were the only two in the room. I was relieved when they finally left, but perplexed by my dad's reaction.

The following day I received an unexpected visit from another group of strange visitors. There was a light knock on the door, and one by one, five blue Smurfs strolled into my hospital room. They looked exactly like they did on one of my favorite cartoons from childhood, except they were dressed in police uniforms. They were pretending to be officers from my division, but they clearly were not. They gathered around my bed and started conversing about what was happening at the station and on the streets. Their voices sounded familiar, and they knew a lot of personal details about me, my job as a police officer, and my accident, but how? I politely waited for them to stop speaking before I said, "Hey, y'all look just like Smurfs!" They laughed in unison, but I didn't think it was funny at all. So I just stared at them quietly until they decided to leave. After a few more equally weird episodes, the doctors lowered the dosage of the morphine and gradually weaned me off of it completely.

Three weeks after being admitted to the ICU, my condition improved enough for me to be moved into a regular room at Memorial Hermann Hospital. I was much more alert and aware; it felt like a fog had been lifted. My thoughts were clear, and I could finally have meaningful dialogue with the doctors, nurses, and hospital staff about my treatment and recovery plan. I was still being fed through the tube in my nose and the pain was still off the charts, but I was glad to be free from the confines of the ICU. There were far more rules and restrictions in the ICU than in the other parts of the hospital. Now I was allowed to have visitors more frequently, and they weren't required to wear hospital gowns and masks when they entered my room.

One afternoon my father thought it would be a good idea to take me for a walk outside. He thought the fresh air and interaction with others might do me some good. Being moved from the bed to the wheelchair was a horribly painful experience. It took four or five nurses to hoist me up and out of the hospital bed like a baby and prop up my limp body in the wheelchair. Every touch sent sharp pains through my body, as though I were being stabbed repeatedly. It was extremely painful, and I hated the indignity of the entire process. Riding in the wheelchair was uncomfortable, but I was glad to be out of my hospital bed. I was bored to death with counting the dots on the ceiling and watching hour after hour of mind-numbing television. When the hospital doors opened, I was blinded by the sun, and it took my eyes a few moments to adjust. It had been several weeks since I'd been outside. I just sat in my chair taking it all in for several minutes. I stared at the trees and bathed in the sun. I couldn't get enough of feeling the breeze against my skin. It was then that I realized just how much I'd taken the simple things in life for granted.

My prognosis was still grim. It was still too early to tell the extent to which I would recover, if at all. Doctors decided it would be best for me to transfer to the spinal cord injury center at The Institute for Rehabilitation and Research at Memorial Hermann (TIRR) so I could work with a team of doctors, nurses, therapists, and other hospital staff who specialized in caring for patients with spinal cord injuries like mine. There were two things standing between me and the transfer to TIRR. I had to wait for a room to become available, and more important, I had to pass a swallow study before I could be released from the hospital. Waiting for a room was easy, but passing the swallow test was harder than I expected. The purpose of the swallow study was to ensure that food was properly going into my stomach and not my airway, which is called aspiration. Additionally, I had to be able to chew and swallow food for nourishment because my NG feeding tube had to be removed before I moved to TIRR. The test was conducted in the X-ray department. They put me in an X-ray machine and placed a piece of graham cracker in my mouth. I chewed it as much as I could and attempted to swallow, but I couldn't get it down. Almost the entire cracker remained in my mouth. I returned to my room, devastated by my latest setback, and cried for hours. I was tired of lying on my back, depending on others to handle my every need. I was eager to get to TIRR so I could at least try to get better, but after failing the swallow study, walking again was laughable. How would I ever walk again if I couldn't even manage to swallow a tiny piece of food?

I was on an emotional roller coaster. Some days were better than others. I tried to remain faithful and optimistic about my future, but the stress of failing the swallow test opened the floodgates, and all the negative emotions I had done my best to repress surfaced and came crashing down on me like a ton of bricks. I was overwhelmed with sadness for the next several days. In retrospect, it was the first time I actually acknowledged my grief. From the moment the car landed in the ditch, I had been so focused on surviving that I hadn't had time to mourn the tragic loss of my former life. The Jason I knew died the day of my accident, and I didn't recognize the helpless man in this broken body. My sadness morphed into anger as I thought about all the things that had been taken from me. Paralysis robbed me of everything I cherished, everything that defined me as a man. Everything I'd worked a lifetime to build and achieve had been snatched from me in an instant. My independence, mobility, and career had vanished into thin air. I couldn't parent or provide for my son, take care of myself, or even swallow food or wipe my own behind. I was mad at the world. I was mad at the suspect for leading me on a high-speed chase. I was mad at myself for chasing him into the darkness. And I was mad at God for letting it all happen. As a child I was taught not to question God, but I couldn't help but ask the question, "Why, Lord?" I needed answers! If God was all knowing, why didn't He warn me and keep me from making that last traffic stop? If He was all powerful, why hadn't He healed my injuries? What had I done so wrong to warrant such a heinous punishment?

I didn't get the answers I needed, so I decided to use my anger as motivation. I was determined to pass the swallow study so I could move on to the next phase in my recovery. Almost two weeks after I failed the first swallow test, they wheeled me back into the room with the X-ray machine and placed another piece of graham cracker in my mouth. I must have chewed that cracker at least a hundred times before I tried to swallow it. I was thrilled when I felt it slide down my throat. I'd overcome the first of many challenges I would face on my road to recovery. Shortly after I passed the swallow test, a room at TIRR became available. I was ready to begin the rehabilitation process. I didn't know if I'd ever get my life back, but I was determined to try.

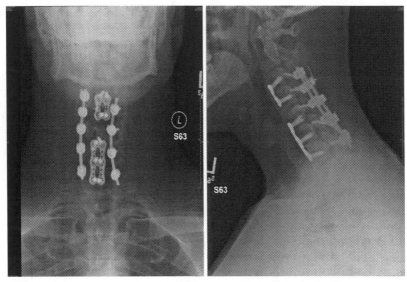

*Front and side views of Jason's neck after surgery*
*Vertebrae C3-C7 were fused together*

*Jason holding his son Jadon one month before the accident*

# ANSWERED PRAYERS

Jesus replied, "I tell you the truth, if you have faith
and do not doubt, not only can you do what was
done to the fig tree, but also you can say to this
mountain, 'Go, throw yourself into the sea' and
it will be done. If you believe, you will receive
whatever you ask for in prayer."

— Matthew 21:21

When I walked out of TIRR nearly two decades earlier, I never imagined in my wildest dreams that I'd ever have to return as a patient. What were the odds I'd find myself back in the same rehabilitation hospital, suffering from injuries sustained in yet another car accident? Was this really happening to me again? Life seemed so unfair. The paramedics escorted me into the hospital through the back entrance and into a large cargo elevator. As we exited the elevator on the fourth floor, the sights, sounds, and smells instantly triggered memories of my past experience at TIRR. Although there had been a lot of renovations and improvements to the building, everything about the hospital was surprisingly familiar.

Seventeen years earlier I had arrived at TIRR as an immature fifteen-year-old boy with two broken legs and a shattered pelvis. I remembered feeling like my life was over. I thought about how much I had dreaded living in a rehabilitation hospital and how I had wanted to go home and have my old life back. Not being able to go to school with my friends or play baseball had felt like the end of the world.

Now, as the nurses wheeled my paralyzed body down the hallway, I would have given anything to trade places with that teenage boy. A few broken bones paled in comparison to the obstacles I was facing. The young boy from the past could move his arms, feed himself, and sit upright without assistance. The doctors were optimistic that his bones would heal properly and he'd walk again. I couldn't do any of those things, and the doctors were uncertain if I'd ever have anything resembling a normal life again.

My trip down memory lane was abruptly interrupted when the nurses pushed me into a double room. There wasn't another patient in the room when I arrived, but the two beds were a clear indication that someone else was on his way. My heart sank at the thought of having a roommate. I was still coming to terms with my injuries and adjusting to the limitations of my paralysis. Depending on others to meet my every need stripped me of every shred of dignity I had. The last thing I needed or wanted was for another person to witness me in my most vulnerable state. I needed my privacy. If I was going to remain at TIRR indefinitely, there was no way I could share such a small, cramped space with another person. I wasn't mentally prepared to coexist with anyone else. Dealing with the doctors and nurses throughout the day and night depleted the little energy I had. I didn't want to be bothered with anyone else. I wanted to be left alone to focus on my recovery. I immediately requested a private room, but it was too late in the day for me to be moved, so I was forced to accept the less-than-ideal situation for the time being. I didn't know when the unwelcomed stranger would show up, so I decided to enjoy the peace and quiet of living alone for as long as I could.

As soon I woke up the next morning, I asked to speak with the floor nurse in charge so I could request a private room. A blonde lady with bright green scrubs and strong perfume entered the room. She introduced herself as Kaki and told me there weren't any private rooms available. I pleaded my case and begged her to move me as soon as possible. She seemed to understand my plight and said she'd complete the necessary paperwork and move me into my own room as soon as one became available. The prospect of sharing such a tiny, overcrowded room with a stranger only added to my growing frustration. I wanted to get up and walk out, but that wasn't happening, so I did the only thing I could do and continued to lie on my back. I was going to have to share Room 401 for a while, and there was nothing I could do about it. I stared at the walls and ceiling, wondering how my life had taken such a turn for the worse. How had I gone from being a strong, active, healthy police officer and father to a feeble, weak, inanimate object? I didn't feel like a person any more. I was like another piece of furniture in the room, but unlike the furniture, I was useless.

I felt myself becoming overwhelmed with negative emotions. I didn't want to break down, so I decided to watch some television and relax. I scanned the room with my eyes, but there wasn't a remote control anywhere to be seen. The televisions were attached to metal arms that extended high above my bed, and I couldn't lift my arm to reach the power button. Once again I was completely helpless. I was too frustrated to call for help, so I stared at the ceiling until I drifted off to sleep.

My first few days at TIRR were filled with interviews by the doctors, nurses, and administrative personnel. I was anxious to start the rehabilitation process, but I was still waiting to be moved to a private room and preoccupied with the possibility of getting a roommate. Fortunately they hadn't assigned another patient to my room, but notion that at any moment I could have to share such a small space was nerve-racking. The doctors' first priority was to thoroughly assess my injuries and condition so they could develop a personalized program to address my specific issues. I was heavily medicated, sedated, and on a ventilator most of the time I was a patient at Memorial Hermann Hospital. It wasn't until I was transferred to TIRR that I was able to fully process and understand the magnitude of my injuries. I knew the paperwork and tests were necessary, but all I really wanted to do was sleep. I was still in a tremendous of amount of pain, and the short ride from the main hospital to TIRR had worn me out. I was exhausted and tried to rest, but every time I dozed off, someone would wake me up to check my vitals, ask more questions, or take a sample of blood for another test.

I met with my team of doctors and physical therapists to discuss my prognosis and treatment plan. Listening to a group of medical professionals explain that I might not regain the full activity of my limbs was almost as painful as the accident that caused my condition. Their grim predictions stole the little hope I had of returning to my old life. I was trapped in my body and didn't know if I would ever be released from the bondage. It felt like there were invisible straps across my legs, torso, and arms that prevented me from making even the slightest movement on my own. Just weeks earlier I had been a healthy, strong, independent active police officer living life on my terms, and now I was reduced to a shell of my former self and had to rely on others to meet every one of my needs. I wasn't in control of my life, and I felt like a child, not a man. I was humiliated, broken, and hopeless. I had spent the last several weeks fighting to stay alive, and now I was questioning the quality of life I would have if my condition did not improve.

After the initial evaluation was complete, I received my daily schedule. My days started with breakfast at eight o'clock and were filled with physical and occupational therapy, group sessions, and other activities until at least five o'clock in the afternoon. Attending therapy and going to class was my new full-time job. I spent my days grinding and working toward something worth much more than a paycheck. I was working to earn my life back. The days were long and difficult, but I forced myself to believe it would all be worth it when I learned to move and walk again. The late Frederick Douglass said, "If there is no struggle, there is no progress." I was definitely struggling and praying for any sign of progress. My ultimate goal was to walk again, but after several weeks of total paralysis, I'd be satisfied with the ability to simply scratch my nose or raise my hand.

The thin curtain that surrounded my side of the room barely shielded me from the lights in the hallway and did absolutely nothing to keep out the constant noise. The noise was so distracting that I never got a good night's sleep. Every night I was awakened by the continuous chatter in the halls. All night long I heard the nurses talking amongst themselves about the patients as well as gossiping about their personal lives. I could hear the hospital doors opening and closing as the doctors and nurses ventured in and out of the other patients' rooms, and the sounds of the stands carrying their laptops and other equipment rolling down the hallway. Most nights I would lie awake, quietly eavesdropping on the doctors' conversations. I listened closely, hoping to hear anything related to me or my prognosis. My attempts at gathering information were unsuccessful. I couldn't understand the medical jargon, and the doctors and nurses never referred to patients by name. The entire fourth floor was dedicated to treating spinal cord injuries, so it was difficult to determine which of us they were discussing. I wished I could get up and shut the door or put my head under the covers to drown out the noise, but I couldn't. I hated not having control over my body or surroundings. I was always at the mercy of others.

I made sure the curtain that acted as a divider between the two sides of the room was pulled out as far as it could go at all times. The curtain was the only thing that separated me from the rest of the world. My roommate still hadn't arrived, and I didn't want to be disturbed whenever he did. One morning shortly after I arrived at TIRR, the curtain swung back without warning. I opened my eyes and was shocked to see several men and women surrounding the foot of my bed. Some were wearing white coats, and others had on scrubs. They were all holding clipboards and taking notes. A gentleman in a white coat stepped forward and introduced himself as Dr. Jeffrey Berliner. We exchanged greetings, and he briefly summarized my case to the others, using information he had learned from reading my medical history and the assessment they took when I arrived at TIRR. It was the first time I could recall having an actual conversation with a doctor since my accident. Typically the doctors spoke with my parents about me instead of talking directly to me.

I listened patiently as Dr. Berliner did his best to communicate my diagnosis in a manner I could understand, but I was listening for one thing and one thing only. I needed to hear him say something that would give me at least a glimmer of hope that I'd walk again. When I didn't get the assurance I needed, I began asking him direct questions. "How long will it take for me to fully recover? Will I be able to walk again? When can I return to work? When will I be able to run and play with my son again?" I was eager to get back to the business of raising my son and working the streets as a police officer. I needed Dr. Berliner to tell me those things were not only possible, but probable. Anything less was unacceptable. My questions must have caught him off guard, because he paused for a long time before he replied. The expression on his face screamed "No!" and confirmed my worst fears. I heard sounds coming out of his mouth, but couldn't decipher the words or comprehend their meaning. I felt so defeated that I tuned him out and closed my eyes until he and the others exited my room.

I was at zero, the lowest point on any measuring scale. I was at rock bottom, void of all hope, faith, and optimism. I had absolutely nothing left to give. My body was shackled with heavy chains and locks, and I couldn't find the keys to free myself. My heart was beating and blood flowed through my veins. I was technically alive, but I wasn't living. I merely existed. After Dr. Berliner left my room, I started to ponder the concept of quality of life. What good was it to be alive if every minute of every day was filled with pain and misery? Every day of my life since the accident had been a struggle, and it was becoming increasingly difficult to fight for a life I hated living. The monotony of lying in bed twenty-four hours a day, seven days a week, unable to move and depending on other people for everything was becoming more and more unbearable as the days passed. Not a day went by that I didn't cry tears of sadness, anguish, and despair. I cried because I was in pain. I cried because I missed my son. I cried because I was trapped in a broken body. I cried because I didn't know if I'd ever be able to work and provide for myself and my son again. I cried every night as I replayed the accident over and over and over again. I cried because one stupid traffic stop had cost me my life. I couldn't make sense of it, so all I could do was cry. How did my partner and the two suspects walk away with only minor scratches and bruises? Why did God choose to spare my life but leave me here in such agony? And why wasn't God answering my cries for help? Again, my pleas for answers were disregarded. I listened quietly for hours, but heard no response. I wanted to pull the plug of life out of the wall socket, but I couldn't move. I searched the depths of my soul for some sort of understanding, but there was nothing.

I spoke to God silently through prayer and even yelled at the top of my lungs, but still there was nothing. I desperately banged on His door so that He could open up and embrace me, but He never opened it. I cried out, "Dear God, where are you? You said you would never leave me or forsake me, so where are You, Lord?" Still there was nothing—not even a whisper from Him. Had my heavenly Father really forsaken me? Had he left me alone to deal with the aftermath of the most catastrophic event of my life? I needed to hear from Him. Countless men and women of faith and spiritual leaders stopped by to pray with me and offer their support and encouragement, but no earthly being could satisfy my yearning to hear from my God. Only He could relieve my grief and pain, but He refused. My faith was slipping away, and I felt completely abandoned and rejected. I stopped questioning God and started questioning whether or not there was a God. If there truly was a God, I needed to know where to find Him, because he certainly wasn't in Room 401.

Hours passed, and day turned to night as I lay in bed quietly waiting for a sign from God. I needed reassurance that He was real, but still there was nothing. There was no indication He existed, and if He didn't exist, then He could not have heard my cries. My eyes were swollen and burned from the salty tears streaming down my face. I was emotionally spent and wanted the day to end. I closed my eyes and started to fall asleep when I heard a voice whisper, "God doesn't love you anymore." I was devastated. The voice was deafening and filled with hate. It was so loud and clear, I was convinced someone was in the room with me. I blew into a straw like device attached to my bed to notify the nurses that I needed attention. It was the only way I could call for help. Two minutes later, a nurse entered my room and asked me what I needed. I told her I was hearing loud voices and couldn't sleep. She looked at my chart and gave me a dose of pain medicine. The medication did the trick and put me to sleep, but it was only a temporary fix. The next morning the same voices were waiting to relay the vile message as soon as I opened my eyes. The voices infiltrated every inch of my mind and remained with me every second of the day. They were like unwelcomed house guests who refused to leave. After two days of relentless taunting, the evil voices vanished as quickly and tersely as they had come.

I was thankful the voices were gone, but I was positive they were playing a cruel game of hide-and-seek and would eventually return. I decided to take advantage of the rare quiet time. I closed my eyes and once again submitted to my Father in prayer. I prayed, "Dear God, I know you're out there and have heard my cries. But I don't understand why you haven't responded to my petitions for help. Didn't you save my life after the accident? Were you not the one who saved me from the hands of the powerful enemy that was sent to destroy me? Where are You, Lord? I need you now like I've never needed you before. There is no one else who can deliver me from this mess. Lord, I am standing on and trusting your word. You told me not to worry and to be strong and of good courage, but how can I, Lord? What do I do, Father? My only hope is in you, so please show yourself." I sat in silence for several minutes, patiently waiting just as I had done every other time, but still there was nothing.

I could feel someone standing and breathing over me while I slept. When I opened my eyes, I was staring directly into the eyes of a lady in scrubs. Who was this strange woman at my bedside, and why was she just standing there, watching me sleep? She must have read my mind, because she immediately introduced herself. "Good morning, Mr. Roy, my name is Efe. I will be your nurse during the day." She had an accent and pronounced her name as "Effie." Immediately after Efe introduced herself she opened a red binder and took out a handful of different medications. She told me the names and purposes of each pill as she placed them in my mouth. One by one, I swallowed each of them. After I took all of the tablets, she pulled out a huge syringe full of Lovenox. Efe explained that the Lovenox would be injected into my stomach twice a day to help prevent blood clots. The shot was extremely painful to say the least. I had been looking forward to starting my physical therapy that morning, but now that my stomach was throbbing from the huge needle, I didn't want to leave my bed.

Efe checked my vitals and gave me a brief rundown of what I could expect each day. I was less than thrilled about the morning medication regimen. I never admitted it, but I missed receiving my medication via the IV lines in my arms and legs. It was much easier than swallowing so many pills and being stabbed in the stomach twice a day.

After Efe left the room, a hospital technician named Tammy came into my room to help me get cleaned up and dressed. I was still in pain from the Lovenox shot and didn't want to be touched or moved, but she insisted that I get up. She was very cheerful and did her best to motivate and encourage me. She told me the only way I'd ever get better was to get out of bed and start the work. She reminded me that I would have to push through the pain if I ever wanted to return to a life of fighting crime. I wasn't in the mood for a pep talk, but I also didn't want to be rude. I didn't answer her questions, but I gave her a half smile and nodded in agreement. Tammy returned the smile and went back to preparing me for the day. I winced in pain at every touch, but she did her best to make the experience as comfortable as possible. I'm sure she knew I was embarrassed that I couldn't perform such simple tasks on my own, but she never made me feel like I was handicapped.

Tammy was kind, gentle, and always professional. She fed me breakfast, meticulously wiping my mouth after each bite. After breakfast she brushed my teeth and washed my face. Feeling the cool water on my face was refreshing and invigorating. I was surprised when she placed my feet in a pair of brown compression tights that looked suspiciously like a pair of my grandmother's stockings. She removed my backless hospital gown and space boots and replaced them with a T-shirt, shorts, and a pair of black Jordan running shoes. I hadn't worn regular clothes in weeks. I hadn't been allowed to wear anything except a hospital gown since the night of my car accident and I was glad to finally be rid of it. I didn't feel so much like a patient or victim; I felt like a regular person again. It's amazing how something as simple as an outfit changed my perspective. I guess what they say is true: when you look good, you feel good. I looked and felt better than I had in weeks. I was ready to literally take the next step in my recovery. It was the beginning of a new journey and chapter in my life.

It took four or five nurses to move me from the bed to the wheelchair. It was painful, but my adrenaline was pumping so hard, it took the edge off. After all the straps were fastened and secured, Tammy rolled me down to the gym on the first floor. I was excited to leave my hospital room. I felt like a kid going on a field trip! I started to get nervous when we approached the double doors leading into the gym. Once again, the negative thoughts and questions raced through my mind. What if I couldn't do the exercises? What if I failed? What if I never walked again? I braced myself as Tammy pushed me through the doors. I was pleasantly surprised when I saw a room full of people who looked just like me. Almost everyone was in a wheelchair. Some wore Miami J collars like mine, and others sported halo braces, metal rings around their heads held together with pins and screws. The gym looked like a regular fitness center. It was filled with all of the typical gym equipment. There were multiple cardio machines such as treadmills, stationary bikes, arm bikes, and stair steppers, as well as Smith machines, exercise mats, and other weight machines and equipment. It reminded me of my old days in the gym. Before my accident I was a true gym rat. I worked out at least five days a week, sometimes twice a day. I lived for the rush I felt after a good workout. I was ready to do whatever it took to get that old feeling back.

As I waited to meet my therapist, I thought about my son. Jadon was my most significant source of strength and inspiration. I wanted to walk again for myself, but I needed to do it for my son. He deserved a dad who could teach him to walk, run, and play sports. I wanted to be able to take him fishing and teach him

81

how to swim and ride a bike. There were many things I wanted to do with my son, and they all revolved around me being able to walk again. More than a month had passed since my accident and my son was growing and developing at what seemed like lightning speed. He was now eight months old and reaching new milestones every day. He learned to crawl while I was in the hospital, and I knew it wouldn't be long before he was walking. I was overcome with a sense of urgency. I never shared it with anyone, not even my physical therapists, but in that moment I set a personal goal for myself. I wanted to learn to walk again before Jadon did. I envisioned the two of us walking side by side. I wanted to be able to stand next to him and hold his hand as he took his first step. My daydream was interrupted when my physical therapist, Kristin, walked over and introduced herself. She wore a huge smile and had a bubbly personality. She had a slim yet athletic build. The muscles in her arms were well defined, and she appeared to be in excellent shape. I was confident she was the right person for the job. If she couldn't teach me to walk again, I didn't know who could. She took me on a tour of the gym and explained each of the machines. Before we started my workout, we sat and discussed her expectations. She took charge of the situation and was very matter of fact about her plan of care for me. She gave me a list of clearly defined goals and details on how we would accomplish each one. As my physical therapist, Kristin was focused on restoring movement and mobility to the lower half of my body. I was impressed by her confidence. Kristin was firm but fair. She was attentive, friendly, and genuine. We had an instant connection. I trusted her implicitly and immediately felt comfortable around her. I truly believed I could attain my goals if I followed her instructions.

I thought maybe she would take it easy on me since it was my first day, but I could not have been more wrong. Time was of the essence; there wasn't a moment to spare. It would take hours of therapy to undo the damage to my body, and there was no time like the present to begin the work! Kristin enlisted the assistance of one of the other therapists to take me out of my wheelchair. They carefully laid me on an exercise mat on the floor and placed my limp body into a safety harness. The harness was connected to a machine that slowly lifted my body off the ground until I was standing up on my feet. It was the first time I had stood up in weeks, and I almost fainted. I felt lightheaded and dizzy. My body had forgotten how it felt to stand. I didn't have any control of my arms and legs, so they just dangled as my body was suspended in the air. I looked like a wet noodle. I was at the very beginning of a lengthy recovery process, but I was excited to be back on my feet. Kristin and I worked together for the longest hour of my life. It seemed like an eternity. I was in pain and covered with sweat, but I still had a full day in front of me

Emily, my occupational therapist, conducted my second therapy session of the day. I was taken aback to see that Emily used a wheelchair, too. We introduced ourselves briefly, and Emily shared her story with me. Several years earlier she was a passenger in a car driven by her boyfriend and wasn't wearing her seat belt. Her boyfriend was speeding and lost control of the car. When it crashed, Emily was thrown through the windshield and landed on her back. I told her how I had been thrown through a windshield as a teenager and was paralyzed as a result of another, more recent car accident. We instantly bonded over the similarities in our stories. It was nice to be in the company of someone who shared my experience. She understood what I had gone through and was living with many of the same limitations I was. I admired Emily's strength and resilient spirit. She was an inspiration to everyone who had the pleasure of making her acquaintance. Watching her move about effortlessly in her wheelchair, helping others, was truly inspirational. She didn't seem at all bothered to be using her wheelchair. I was perplexed by how genuinely happy she was.

I didn't understand how she could be so happy, knowing she would likely live the rest of her life in a wheelchair. The prospect of never walking again had sent me into a deep depression. I was extremely curious about the source of her inner peace and joy. I wondered if I'd ever be as comfortable in my own skin as Emily seemed to be in hers.

My sessions with Emily focused on exercises designed to help me regain functionality in my upper body. The long-term goal was to help me become as independent as possible. Emily was going to help me learn how to do tasks such as brushing my teeth, and feeding and dressing myself. We started my first occupational therapy session on the functional electrical stimulation bike, or FES. It looked very similar to the arm bikes at a regular gym, except there were several wires attached to it. The FES bike applied small electrical pulses to the paralyzed muscles in my arms to stimulate movement. The electrical current caused my muscles to contract, and the contraction caused my arms to move. These muscle contractions were produced in a specific pattern, which resulted in my arms moving in a pedaling motion on the bike. The FES bike was quite convenient because it didn't require me to be removed from my wheelchair. Emily's assistant locked my arms into place and placed the electrodes, which were small square stickers, over the muscles in my arms. Each electrode was attached to a wire that was connected to a stimulator, the actual machine that produced the current. The assistant flipped the switch, and I immediately felt a tingling sensation on my skin. It felt like I was being pricked in my arms with a thousand tiny pins and needles. I started on the lowest setting, and the intensity was gradually increased until the current was strong enough to make my muscles contract. I was in awe as my arms started moving. It had been weeks since my arms had done anything more than lie or hang lifelessly by my sides. I realized I wasn't actually moving my arms on my own, but seeing them move without the assistance of a nurse or doctor was encouraging. My arms continued to pedal for approximately fifteen minutes. My arms were sore from all the activity, but I was looking forward to trying it again soon.

After a short break, Emily's assistant wheeled me over to the Armeo Spring machine, an ergonomic arm exoskeleton with integrated springs designed to help patients regain active movement of the arm and hand. The metal machine embraced the inner arm from the shoulder to the hand. It was similar to playing a video game, but I could use only one arm at a time. The first time I tried it, I didn't like it because I could barely move my arm. I strained and pushed as hard as I could, but my arm wouldn't move. I was tired and discouraged. Emily tried to make me feel better and said most patients weren't successful the first time they tried to use the machine, but it didn't help. I was drained and just wanted to be left alone. I waited for Emily to dismiss me and waited for Tammy to wheel me back to my room for lunch.

When Tammy and I returned to my room, I was annoyed to find my new roommate and his family. His family members were gathered around his bed, conversing with one another. I was definitely not in the mood to meet new people, so I quietly said hello and continued on to my side of the room. As I passed by his bed, I noticed my new roomie wasn't wearing a neck brace and that he seemed to be a lot younger than me. I wondered what had happened to him and where he was in his recovery. I felt a little better after I rested and had lunch, so I decided to formally introduce myself. His name was Damian, and he was very friendly. His entire family was also warm and inviting. Damian obviously noticed the age difference between us, too, because he referred to me as "sir" a few times. I appreciated how respectful he was, but I was adamant that he not call me sir.

We made casual conversation for a few minutes, but I could tell each of us was curious about what had happened to the other. I shared my story with him and asked him about his injuries.

I was speechless when he told me he had been shot nine times, including once in the center of his chest. I was astounded that he had survived such a horrific incident. I'd spent years working the streets as a police officer and had seen countless of people die from one gunshot wound, let alone nine. I hate to admit it, but I couldn't help but think about the rapper 50 Cent as Damian recounted the events of the night he was shot. He told me he didn't feel any pain when he was shot, but that he immediately realized he couldn't move. His story brought me to tears and triggered memories of my days as a cop. He and his parents started to cry when I told him how it had been my life's dream to protect and serve my community and that I wished I could've been there to save him. It was a beautiful moment that I'll never forget. Our shared experiences connected us on a level that surpassed the age and cultural differences. We were nothing more than two survivors learning to cope and adjust to our new normal.

Damian was truly heaven sent. His uplifting spirit was just as amazing as his story of survival. When I looked into his eyes, I saw hope. I can't explain why, but his mere presence was enough to restore my faith and give me hope that I would walk again. Damian was the answer, the sign from God I'd been waiting for since I arrived. It wasn't a coincidence that he was my roommate. It wasn't a chance meeting that caused us to cross paths. Only God could've orchestrated that moment. I thought about how I had been obstinately opposed to having a roommate and how I had begged to be moved to a private room. If I'd had it my way, I would've been moved to a private room the day I arrived, but God knew I needed to meet Damian. Finally, God showed up in Room 401.

After class I went back to my room and learned my private room was ready. Damian and I had only been roommates for a couple of days, but I had mixed emotions about moving. I was happy I would have my privacy and personal space, but I was certainly going to miss my new buddy, Damian. Fortunately I was moving only a few doors down the hall to Room 404, so Damian and I could keep in touch. My new room was very spacious. I felt like I was in a hotel suite or studio apartment. It had a large couch for visitors, and there was even a small kitchen with a miniature refrigerator to store refreshments. It was more than I'd hoped for and exactly what I needed. I enjoyed having the space and freedom to have more visitors. I liked being surrounded by family and friends. Their love and support motivated me to push myself to the next level. I wanted to make them proud. Unfortunately, too much of anything isn't good. I had visitors around the clock. It seemed like there was someone in my room twenty-four hours a day. The endless flow of visitors eventually took its toll on me. I couldn't get any rest, and I felt tired all the time. I was thankful to everyone for taking time to check on me, but some days, I was in so much pain and so exhausted, I just didn't want to be bothered. I didn't want to be rude or hurt anyone's feelings by asking them to leave or not come, but I started to become concerned when I was too tired to give 100 percent in therapy because I hadn't gotten enough sleep the day before. The visits were also emotionally taxing, because many times I was confronted with questions for which I had no answer. I didn't know if I would ever walk again, and I certainly didn't know if I'd return to the Houston Police Department. Conversing with my colleagues about work and listening to my friends discuss their professional lives forced me to deal with the uncertainty of my future. I had defined myself as a police officer for years, and now I had no idea who I was or what I would do with my life.

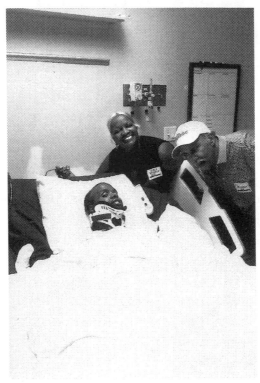

*Jason with his parents at TIRR*

*Jason holding his son Jadon for the first time after the accident*

# 9 A GLIMPSE OF HOPE

> He said to the paralytic, "I tell you, get up, take
> your mat and go home." He got up, took his mat
> and walked out in full view of them all. This amazed
> everyone and they praised God, saying, "We have
> never seen anything like this!"
>
> —Mark 2:11–12

I was in the beginning stages of my recovery and cautiously optimistic about how much function and mobility I would regain. I was excited about every accomplishment, no matter how small, but I wasn't going to be satisfied until I walked out of TIRR on my own. Just thinking about how far I had to go to reach my goal was exhausting. I still couldn't move on my own and required constant assistance to do everything. I was determined to get better, but some days the physical pain overshadowed my determination. It had been more than six weeks since my accident, and I was still in immeasurable amounts of pain. Some days were better than others, but the pain was worst in the evenings when I tried to sleep. Every night I was awakened by a burning sensation all over my body. It felt like fire was coursing through my veins. The pain medication took the edge off, but nothing completely eliminated the pain. I tried everything imaginable to take my mind off it. I meditated, prayed, and even tried breathing and relaxation techniques, but nothing helped. I didn't want the doctors to increase the dosage of the pain pills because I needed to be as alert and aware as possible for physical therapy and my other classes. So, I did what I had to do and learned to live with the pain. It wasn't easy, but I didn't have a choice. I could lie in bed and cry or get up and do the work. Either way I was going to be in pain, so I decided I should at least have something to show for it.

Learning to live with the physical pain and limitations was only half the battle. I still had to deal with the emotional aspect of my injuries. When I arrived at TIRR, I was a broken man in every sense. My body, mind, and soul were all shattered. The doctors and therapists were tasked with healing my body, but I had to mend my spirit. I was still searching for the purpose behind my pain. My faith in God had been restored, but I still didn't know why He had allowed me to be so badly injured while others walked away with only scratches and bruises. I needed answers. Each evening I would lie in bed, staring at the newspaper clippings taped to my window to block the sun, and meditate for at least an hour, sometimes longer. I didn't want anyone or anything to distract me from hearing the voice of God. I didn't know when He would answer, but I had faith that He would.

Late one evening after one of my more trying days of therapy, the Lord revealed Himself to me. He assured me the pain and suffering would not last forever, and told me He had a plan and purpose for my life. He explained that He hadn't allowed my accident to happen to me, but that He had chosen me to be an earthly vessel to carry out His work. In that moment I realized that everything I was going through was much bigger than me. I didn't fully understand God's vision for my life, but I knew I had a purpose and that my struggle was not in vain. I still battled feelings of sadness, frustration, and depression, but knowing God had a purpose for my life gave me the strength I needed to push through the pain and forge ahead on my road to recovery.

One of the highlights of moving from Memorial Hermann to TIRR was having my son visit me. He was too young to come to the intensive care unit, and I wasn't in any condition to visit with him at that time. Jadon was my inspiration and motivation to live. He was my life. From the moment I found out my girlfriend, Angel, was expecting, everything I did was for him. Angel and I moved in together and I started working long hours to provide a comfortable life for us. I was with him every day of his life until the accident, so being separated from him for more than a month was extraordinarily difficult. I was so excited the first day his mother brought him to visit me. I thought spending time with my son would give me the extra boost of energy I needed to get through the tough days ahead. When his mom walked through the door with him, my eyes filled with tears of joy. I was so happy to see him, I could hardly contain myself. When she propped him up on my lap, I wanted to hug him, but I couldn't move my arms. Once again I was reminded how big the "little things," such as giving your loved ones a hug, are when you lose them. I looked over every inch of his little body. I couldn't believe how much he'd grown and changed in a month. I was shocked when he started to cry and reach for his mother. The frightened look on his face broke my heart. The big brown eyes that used to light up every time they saw me stared blankly at me as if I were a stranger. Watching my son turn away from me and scream was more painful than any physical ailment I'd endured. I knew I had to rebuild my body, but I never thought in a million years I'd have to rebuild my relationship with my son. He was all I had left. Jadon was the one constant in my life, and it seemed as if I'd lost him. My accident and injuries had stolen everything that was precious to me, but I was not going to let them take away my baby too. As the days and weeks passed, his mother continued to bring him to visit. Eventually we reconnected and reestablished our unbreakable bond. I promised myself and my son that I would do whatever it took to get Daddy home!

It took me about a week to begin adjusting to living at TIRR. I was starting to let my guard down and slowly but surely build relationships with my therapists and the other patients. After I moved into my private room, my family decorated it with pictures and a few other personal items to make it feel more like home. And there was nothing like being able to have a hot plate of ox tails, candied yams, green beans and corn bread from my favorite soul food restaurant, Mama's Oven to make me feel right at home. That was the first thing I craved when I was able to eat real food. All I wanted was some smothered oxtails with rice, candied yams, and a side of green beans.

There were also several pictures of me from before my accident. At first it was hard to look at them because they were a reminder of everything I had been and all the things I wasn't any more. But eventually I stopped focusing on what I had lost and used the old photographs as motivation for what I hoped to become. My favorite pictures were the ones of my son. Every time I felt down or wanted to give up, I looked across the room at his picture and remembered my promise to him. My parents also brought me my cell phone. I was astonished at the number of missed calls and voice mail messages. There were so many missed calls that the numbers were no longer registering on the phone and my mailbox was filled to capacity. I was overwhelmed with gratitude and felt the love as I listened to each voice mail message and read every text message. It was surreal to know that hundreds, possibly thousands, of people were praying on my behalf. My cell phone started ringing the moment I turned it on and did not stop until I turned it off each night. I missed most of my incoming calls because my right arm wasn't strong enough to pick up the phone and I couldn't move my left arm at all. Making phone calls wasn't a walk in the park either, but it was great exercise for strengthening my right arm. I used the fingers on my right hand to dial the number and select the speakerphone option. It would take me a few minutes, but eventually I could push the phone onto my chest and let it sit there for the duration of the conversation. The long process required to make a phone call, an ordinarily simple task, was another example of how much my life had changed and how much I had taken for granted before my injuries.

At least one police officer was stationed at my hospital room door at all times, and I was escorted by another officer every time I left my room. I appreciated having the support of my fellow officers, but I later learned their presence stirred up a considerable amount of drama. Rumors that I was an inmate started circulating around the hospital. I was both surprised and offended at the assumption, but it made sense after I heard stories about how some of the other patients were injured. There were all kinds of people at TIRR. Some had been born with debilitating injuries, and others had been hurt while committing violent crimes. It was amazing how sharing similar physical injuries and struggles bonded us in spite of the extreme differences in our backgrounds. The very kinds of people I used to arrest were now sitting next to me, learning to walk and live again. It was amazing. TIRR provided a comfortable environment where we were free to live unashamed of our injuries. It was the only place where using a wheelchair was normal. One of my favorite things about living at TIRR was the functional group class. The class met Monday through Friday, for one hour each day. Everyone in my class was either a paraplegic or suffering from tetraplegia, paralysis caused by illness or injury that causes partial or total loss of use of all their limbs and torso. I was admittedly standoffish when I started the class. My invisible wall of protection was still up, and I wasn't particularly interested in making new friends. I participated in the group activities, but I was reluctant to open up to the others. The other patients in the class shared stories about their injuries and families, but I didn't talk much the first few days. I needed time to take it all in and feel everyone out.

Mr. Jim was the most memorable person in the class. Both of his legs had been amputated, and he had only nubs for fingers. Mr. Jim's personality was larger than life. He had one of the kindest, most jovial spirits I've ever encountered. His laugh was loud and infectious. No matter how bad I felt, I started to smile and feel better the moment I laid eyes on Mr. Jim. He told the most hilarious stories and kept everyone laughing at his crazy jokes. He was the life of our functional group class! I can't recall a time when I saw him sad or discouraged. It was as if he was immune to negativity. He chose to be happy and live a full life in spite of his disabilities. Mr. Jim inspired me to stop throwing my personal pity parties for one and start appreciating all the things I had. Although they didn't work as well as they had before, I still had my arms, legs, fingers, and toes. More important, I was alive. And as long as I was alive, I had the potential to recover.

The functional group class was designed to help us retrain our limbs that were damaged as a result of the spinal cord injury. We worked diligently to learn to perform basic tasks such as writing, turning pages in books, using the telephone, and typing. I was focused on regaining mobility and strengthening both of my arms. During one of my first classes I asked for a pen and paper and tried to write, but I couldn't. I was barely able to grip the pen and move it along the paper, and I couldn't write legible letters or numbers. I was like a young child first learning to write. I was discouraged, but determined. Learning to write was just as important as learning to walk again. I continued to work on holding a pen and learning to write again in class, and I even spent time practicing in my room. Each day I went through countless sheets of paper as I scribbled my name over and over again. After a few weeks of practicing, the letters started to become more and more legible. I was able to print and sign my name. Ironically, my penmanship actually improved from how it had been before the accident. I guess the old saying "perfect practice makes perfect" is true.

The instructors of the functional group classes taught us to play games and sports activities that forced us to use our affected limbs, thereby strengthening them in the process. My favorite game was volleyball. Watching six adults in wheelchairs play volleyball was quite a sight. We used balloons instead of balls and rackets for our hands to hit them across the net. Before my accident I lived a very active life. I'd been an athlete since grade school, so I felt at home in the gym. Maneuvering my wheelchair across the gymnasium was a challenge at first, but eventually I got the hang of it and really started to enjoy playing the games. We also took several field trips. We went to the mall, restaurants, and other places around the city. In fact, my first outing after my accident was with my classmates. They loaded us into vans and drove us to the Galleria, the largest mall in Houston. I was nervous about going out in public, and a little embarrassed about being out in a wheelchair wearing my not-so-stylish Miami J collar and compression tights, but having my new friends there to support me helped ease my anxiety.

I was learning to live with my disabilities, but the one thing I never adjusted to was the total loss of independence and privacy. I hated being treated like a baby, but the reality was that I needed other people to live. I couldn't do anything on my own. I couldn't feed or dress myself, and worst of all, I couldn't use the restroom without assistance. A week after I arrived at TIRR, I started my bowel program. The paralysis caused by my spinal cord injury damaged the nerves that control my bowel. As a result, I no longer felt the urge to "go" when my rectum was full of waste, nor did I have the ability to push the feces out. In an effort to prevent me from having accidents and to keep my bowel from becoming impacted, I had to follow a strict program so the nurses could empty my bowel and manually remove the stool on a schedule. It was the single most degrading experience of my life and the worst part of being paralyzed. I made up every excuse in the book to delay the process, but no matter how much I tried to procrastinate, the nurses made sure I followed my program. Every night, seven days a week, I was turned on my side (in my hospital bed) and a suppository was inserted into my rectum. The nurse would wait about fifteen minutes to allow the stimulant to work before she used her fingers to stimulate my bowel and manually remove the feces. The entire process was demeaning and physically draining. It never got any easier and was equally as embarrassing every time. The inability to control my bowel movements made me feel like less than a man. I had never felt more vulnerable and powerless. Besides being extremely humiliating it was incredibly painful. The nurses wore latex gloves and used a lubricant, but that didn't prevent them from scratching me occasionally. It felt like they were scraping out my insides with a knife. The pain was so unbearable, I would ask the nurses to put my sheet or pillowcase in my mouth so I could clench down on it and avoid screaming at the top of my lungs. I tried to zone out and think about anything other than what was going on at the time, but I was so uncomfortable that all I could do was stare at the wall and cry.

I participated in the bowel program for about three weeks, until I couldn't stand it any longer. The nurses offered me an enema instead. Receiving an enema was a welcomed alternative. Enemas were much less invasive than digital stimulation and manual removal; however, they triggered immediate results and caused me to defecate on myself because I couldn't move to the commode fast enough. I was horrified every time it happened. I knew preventing the accidents was beyond my control, but I was still ashamed. I was so embarrassed that I refused to make eye contact with the nurses when they came in to clean up the mess. After more than a few of these embarrassing mishaps, I requested that a bedpan be placed underneath me before I was given the enema. Using the bedpan wasn't the most pleasant experience, but it was far better than pooping all over myself and my bed.

In addition to not having the sensation to have bowel movements, I wasn't able to urinate on my own. The nurses used an intermittent catheter to drain my bladder every four to six hours. Being catheterized was almost as painful and horrendous as the bowel program. The process was excruciating. The nurses inserted a thin metal tube into the urethra through my penis. Once again, I was stripped of my manhood and dignity, and all I could do was cry out in pain. To make matters worse, I also developed several urinary tract infections. The infections were even more painful than the catheterization. I felt the constant urge to urinate and a relentless burning sensation in my penis. It was the absolute worst. Going to the restroom on my own was another one of those "little things" I learned to appreciate and longed to do on my own again.

After two weeks at TIRR, I had become acclimated to my new environment and daily routine. I was focused on going to therapy and the group sessions with other patients. My days were always long, but I didn't mind. I was determined to reach my ultimate goal of walking again. I did my best to keep my eye on the prize and focus on my recovery, but sometimes it was difficult to remain motivated. Every aspect of the healing process seemed almost as painful as my actual injuries. When I started my journey, I had no idea how much worse things would become before they got better. One of the most memorable examples of the pain of healing was the day Dr. Berliner removed the stitches from my scalp and neck. I had been sedated for all of my surgeries, and didn't anticipate the pain involved in taking out more than fifty stitches. I winced as he carefully removed each one. Some came out more easily than others, but more often than not, Dr. Berliner had to yank them out. He applied topical pain medication, but it didn't help at all. Halfway through, I thought I was going to pass out from the pain and begged him to take a break. The pain was so great that it reminded me of how I felt when I was trapped in my police car. My head was throbbing, and sharp pains shot through my neck and back. I cringed, and tears fell from my eyes as he removed the remaining stitches. It was just one more part of the painful healing process.

When I first arrived at TIRR, I felt a sense of satisfaction every time I reached a new milestone. Anything was better than being stuck in ICU; however, after a couple of weeks of little to no progress in my condition, I became very discouraged. My family, friends, and therapists were my biggest cheerleaders and always had encouraging words for me, but sometimes it wasn't enough. Some days I had to dig deep within and encourage myself. On my toughest days I thought about an article I read about one of my sports heroes, Michael Jordan. Jordan is hailed as the greatest professional basketball player of all time. In the article he said he had missed more than nine thousand shots in his career. He had lost almost three hundred games, and he had been trusted twenty-six times to take the game-winning shot and missed. He said he had failed numerous times in his life, but that his failures were the reasons he succeeded.

I also spent a lot of time thinking about Nicholas James Vujicic. I hadn't heard of him before my accident, but a friend showed me several videos of his motivational speeches. Mr. Vujicic was born without arms or legs. In one of the segments I watched, he talked about falling down in life and the importance of getting back up when you fall. His message was simple, yet powerful. Along the way in life we will all likely encounter obstacles that cause us to feel discouraged. Many times the challenges we face will seem insurmountable and make us feel like we're too weak to get back up and press forward toward our dreams and goals. It is in those difficult times that we must find the strength within ourselves to get back up and try again. He taught me no matter how many times I fall down I should continue to get back up and try again, because as long as I continue to try there is always the possibility of success and a chance things will get better. I was blown away by his story and zest for life. Like Mr. Jim, Mr. Vujicic had no arms or legs, but he didn't let his differences keep him from living a meaningful, productive life. He didn't use his disabilities as an excuse to be defeated or discouraged. After I watched his video, I thought about how ungrateful I had been. I had spent so much time and energy focused on what I didn't have that I hadn't taken the time to truly thank God for sparing my life. Most people would not have survived such a catastrophic accident, but I did. Not only did I survive, but I made it out with all of my limbs intact. For the first time since my accident, I truly thanked God for saving my life and asked Him to forgive me for being so unappreciative of all His blessings.

I applied the lessons I learned from Michael Jordan and Nicholas James Vujicic to my recovery. I changed my perspective and started to view my failures as learning opportunities to help me get closer to my ultimate goal of walking again. Knowing that one of the world's greatest athletes and a man born without limbs had tried and failed countless times gave me the confidence I needed to get back up and try again. My faith rose to a higher level, and I refused to let doubt and defeat rule my life. I had mountain-moving faith that I would walk again. I declared that God would heal me and spoke victory and a full recovery over my body. Every time I started to feel discouraged, I would quietly repeat, "I will not be defeated. I will walk again." I didn't have the physical strength to pick up my Bible, but God put one special Scripture on my heart. Every day I meditated on 1 Peter 1:6–7: "In this you greatly rejoice, though now for a little while you may have to suffer grief in all kinds of trials. These have come so that your faith of greater worth than gold, which perishes even though refined by fire, may be proved genuine and may result in praise, glory and honor when Jesus Christ is revealed." This Scripture taught me that God never said I wouldn't face trials and tribulations; in fact, He knew that I would. But the good news is that He promised my suffering wouldn't last forever.

I trusted God's word and believed He would heal me. Even if I wasn't physically as strong as I had been in the past, I was confident God would render me a better man if I remained faithful and did the work. As my faith and confidence grew, my doubt disappeared. My light started to shine again, and everyone noticed. I was much happier and had a brighter outlook on my life and future. I continued to strive toward my goals, but I also appreciated the blessings I already had. I had finally found the same peace that allowed people like Emily and Jim to live happy, fulfilling lives.

Shortly after my epiphany, or as Oprah calls it, my "aha moment," I started to notice signs of improvement in my condition. It happened the first time I was hooked up to the Transcutaneous Electrical Nerve Stimulation Machine, or TENS unit. TENS is a method of therapy used to treat patients with acute and chronic pain. The small, battery-operated machine delivers low-voltage electrical impulses into the body that should feel like a pleasant tingling sensation in the areas affected by the pain. While I was hooked up to the TENS machine, I looked down and saw the fingers on my left hand move. I knew it wasn't a voluntary movement, but it gave me hope nonetheless. If my fingers were coming back to life, then it was possible for the rest of my body to follow suit. Watching my body respond to the therapy motivated me to push myself past my limits. Each time I reached a new milestone, I challenged myself to surpass it. I would get frustrated when my nurses were even a few minutes late giving me my medication and preparing me for the day. I was eager to get down to the gym to see if I could do better than I had the previous day. Everything was falling into place. The minute I started to believe in myself, great things started to happen.

I'll never forget the day I moved my right foot on my own. One afternoon while I was alone in my room, I started to stare at my feet. It took a few minutes for me to get the courage to try to move them, because I was afraid of failure. For the first time in several weeks I was in a happy place, but I knew my emotional state was still very fragile. I didn't want to do anything to cause a setback. I continued to stare at my feet as I worked up the nerve to try to wiggle them. I looked around anxiously just to be sure nobody was watching, clenched my teeth, and strained as hard as I could. Nothing! I was a little discouraged and tempted to give up, but I quickly shook off those feelings and tried again. Still there was nothing. I was sweating and extremely tired after my first two failed attempts. Trying to move my feet was surprisingly physically draining. It took several minutes before I had enough energy to try again. I took a deep breath, bit down on my bottom lip, and tried with all my might to move my feet. I was ecstatic and shocked when my right foot moved! I wanted to shout for joy, but I was speechless and exhausted. Happy tears filled my eyes. For weeks I'd felt like I was stuck in a dead body, but suddenly it felt like it was coming back to life! I was so proud and excited that I told and showed anyone and everyone who entered my room. I knew I still had a long road to travel before I could walk again, but moving my right foot made me feel like anything was possible. From that day on, I moved my right foot at least a few times a day. The more I did it, the easier it became to move, and my confidence started to soar. It may have seemed like a small thing to some people, but it was life altering for me. It made me feel powerful and victorious. I knew it was the first of many breakthroughs in my recovery. After I was able to move my right foot on my own, I truly believed the sky was the limit.

Another one of my most memorable days at TIRR was the

first time my therapists put me in the TheraStride Treadmill Machine. The TheraStride Machine is a body-supported treadmill used to train paralyzed patients to stand and walk again. When I first learned I would be using the machine, I was excited at the proposition of standing and walking again, but also nervous because I didn't know what to expect. It took a team of therapists to secure my limp body in the harness. One of the technicians, Willie, must have noticed the panicked look on my face, because he looked at me with a huge grin and asked, "Are you ready?"

I shook my head and replied, "Do I have a choice?" They all laughed, and I took a deep breath and braced myself. I prayed the harness wouldn't break and send me crashing to the floor. As soon as they turned the machine on, my legs started to move beneath me. I was shocked! How in the world were my legs moving when I was completely paralyzed? Two minutes earlier I had been sitting in my wheelchair, unable to move, and now I was walking. I honestly couldn't believe it. My parents joined me for my therapy session that day, and the looks on their faces were priceless. Their eyes were so wide, I thought they might pop out of the sockets, and their mouths fell open in disbelief. It was so unbelievable; I actually thought I was dreaming.

I continued to walk for several minutes before I asked them to stop the machine. I needed a moment to compose myself and process the fact that I had just walked on a treadmill. Everyone in the gym was smiling, and some were even clapping. I turned to one of the technicians and asked, "Was that me or the machine?"

He quickly replied, "It was all you, Jason." I tried to be strong, but I couldn't contain the tears of joy. I appreciated him giving me the credit and was thoroughly impressed by the machine; however, I knew a higher power greater than me or any machine was at work. I knew from where my strength cometh. I closed my eyes and thanked God for what He had done and what I knew He would continue to do in my life.

June 13, 2011, was the first day I stood on my own. It started out just like any other day. I woke up, took my medication, got dressed, and had breakfast before going to the gym for physical therapy. While Kristin, my therapist, was assisting me with my stretching exercises, she said I should try standing on my own. I was excited, but afraid that I might fall and injure myself even more. As soon as we were finished stretching, Kristin lifted me out of my wheelchair and helped me stand up on a black rubber mat. She held on to my arm long enough for me to get my bearings before she let go and stepped away from the mat. I was shocked that I was able to continue standing without assistance. It was more than just an accomplishment. It was a miracle. I was able to stand for only a few seconds before I had to sit down. I started to feel dizzy and lightheaded because my body wasn't used to being on its feet in an upright position. I fought to hold back the tears of joy. I was elated that my body was slowly but surely coming back to life and hopeful I would continue to see signs of improvement. My left side was still paralyzed. My doctors and therapists were still unsure whether it would respond to the therapy or if I'd ever regain movement in my left arm and leg, but I was no longer concerned with their prognosis. I was thankful for everything they did to help save my life, but I firmly believed God was in control of my life and destiny. If He could perform miracles to save my life and give me feeling and control of the right side of my body, I was confident He would heal me completely and remove the paralysis plaguing my left side.

One week after I stood up on my own, I took my first steps! It happened during one of my physical therapy sessions with Kristin. Words can't explain how I felt. I had wanted to walk again for weeks, and I had finally done it. They weren't very big steps in the physical sense, but to me they were enormous, and in my mind they represented a huge advancement toward my recovery. The first time I walked, I counted five steps before I had to sit down.

My legs had become weak from being immobile for so long. They had to be retrained in every sense of the word. I had to learn how to place one foot in front of the other—a simple task I once took for granted. But as the days passed, I grew stronger, and for the first time I was able to walk to the restroom on my own. It felt good to stand up and urinate rather than pee through a bag or be transferred from a wheelchair to do so. The more I walked around my hospital room, the more confident I became in my ability to do things on my own. Even though I felt a sense of independence, I still had a long way to go. I couldn't allow the unknown to deter me from pushing myself further each day, even if I was in excruciating pain. I was determined to be me again.

Every Friday, my dad and I attended an informal round-table meeting with Dr. Berliner, my primary care physician at TIRR; my occupational and physical therapists; nurse Efe; Michael, my hospital caseworker; and MaryAnn, my city case manager, to discuss the status of my overall condition and progression (or regression) in therapy. My physical therapist would provide detailed updates about the treatments I had received that week and how my body had responded to each one. The occupational therapist reported on how well I was learning to perform everyday activities, such as dressing and bathing myself. I looked forward to the meetings each week. Listening to the doctors and therapists give honest accounts of how well or poorly I was doing, supported by specific examples, helped me better understand my strengths and weaknesses, as well as know which areas I should focus on more to reach my goals.

One Friday in mid-June 2011, I went to what I thought was just another ordinary patient status meeting. As usual, Dr. Berliner went around the table and gave everyone an opportunity to give a brief summary of my progress. The updates were all positive, and my therapists seemed optimistic about my recovery. I was excited to hear I was doing so well, but that excitement was short-lived when I learned I was going to be released from TIRR the following week. Dr. Berliner explained that my inpatient treatment would be ending and that I'd continue my therapy in TIRR's outpatient program at Kirby Glen. I was stunned by the news. For months I had prayed for the day I'd be able to go home, but now that day was on the horizon, and I didn't want to go. Of course there were times when I missed being at home with my family, especially my son, but I had become surprisingly content living at TIRR. I was thriving in the structured yet relaxed environment, and knew that being there was critical to my recovery. Shortly after the meeting with the entire team, I met privately with Dr. Berliner. I told him I wasn't ready to go home and felt very strongly that my recovery would suffer if I was released too soon. I knew I would not continue to progress at the same pace if I was forced to leave TIRR before I was physically and mentally well enough to care for myself. Fortunately, Dr. Berliner and Michael understood my concerns and extended my stay another few weeks.

During the weeks leading up to my release from TIRR, I was filled with mixed emotions. Going home meant I'd see my son every day and regain some of my privacy, and I was happy about that. However, I was extremely anxious about venturing back out into the world as a disabled man. Angel and I were still living together at the time of my release from TIRR, but she wasn't equipped with the skills, nor did she have time to provide me with round the clock care. We never discussed it, but I imagine she was overwhelmed by the thought of having to take care of all of my needs, in addition to being a working mother. My mind was consumed with frightening thoughts of life after TIRR. I had made significant progress in my recovery, but there was a long way to go before I would feel confident enough to live on my own again. I was still in constant pain, as my neck and back was still healing from the surgery. I had only limited mobility in my arms and legs, so I needed assistance with basic tasks such as dressing, showering, and preparing meals. I knew I wasn't well enough to take care of myself. I was afraid to leave the security of the hospital. TIRR was a safe and secure environment equipped with everything I needed to survive and be as comfortable as possible given my physical limitations. As long as I was at the hospital, doctors, nurses, therapists, and other specialists were available twenty-four hours a day, seven days a week to assist me with anything I needed. Who would help me when I went home? Who would have the time, knowledge, and patience to assume the responsibility of my care? I had the support of my friends and family, but they weren't medical professionals trained to treat and care for me like the doctors and nurses at TIRR. Additionally, it was much easier for me to depend on the staff at TIRR than to feel like a burden to my family.

As my release date approached, I started to dread the thought of going home. After I accepted the fact that I had to leave TIRR, I asked MaryAnn to research alternative living arrangements for me. I was willing to do anything and go anywhere to avoid returning to my apartment, even if that meant moving into an assisted-living facility or another inpatient rehabilitation hospital. One afternoon, shortly before I was scheduled to leave TIRR, I confided in my father about my reservations about leaving the hospital. When I admitted I didn't want to go home, he seemed confused and agitated. I felt like he couldn't and didn't understand my feelings, so in that moment I decided I would keep my feelings and concerns to myself. I knew I couldn't run from my problems and fears forever, so I declined an offer to move into an inpatient residential facility and decided I would go home when I left TIRR.

July 7, 2011, the day I was discharged from TIRR, was emotional and bittersweet. Against all odds I walked out through the same sliding glass doors I had been pushed through in my wheelchair so many times before. I was happy I'd reached my goal of walking again, but terrified of the unknown life I was walking toward.

# MY DARKEST HOUR, MY BRIGHTEST DAY

> Then they cried to the Lord in their trouble, and he saved them from their distress. He sent forth his word and he healed them; he rescued them from the grave.
>
> —Psalm 107:19–20

It had been two months since I'd been home, and although things were almost exactly as I'd left them, my apartment felt like a new place. Everything was just as I remembered, with the exception of my new recliner next to the couch. I wasn't strong enough to get up and down without assistance, and the recliner with the lift enabled me to push myself forward until I was able to easily maneuver out of the chair. I tried to be hopeful, but returning home to live was more difficult than I'd imagined. My apartment wasn't outfitted with the conveniences of the hospital. It was nearly impossible for me to navigate through the tight spaces and narrow hallways with a wheelchair, so I was forced to walk, even when I felt like I was in too much pain to move.

The nights were the worst. I was in so much pain and discomfort, I couldn't get any sleep. The plush, comfortable bed

I had missed for months was now the most uncomfortable place in the world. My neck and back were still healing, so lying flat on my back was incredibly painful. I also couldn't sit up on my own from the lying position in the bed because my abdominal muscles were too weak to help raise my upper body. I actually missed my hospital bed. I hoped having one at home would help alleviate some of my issues, but I was wrong. The only positive thing about the hospital bed was that I could raise my head and feet with the remote control, but it didn't help relieve the pain besides it was too small for my six-foot, two-inch frame. There was still too much pressure on my neck and back. I tried positioning pillows behind my neck and under my legs, but nothing I did eased the pain. I was deliriously tired and wanted nothing more than a good night's sleep, but nothing helped.

In addition to the pain, I constantly had the urge to urinate. It was annoying and frustrating. Getting up and walking the short distance to the restroom was difficult and painful. Sometimes the pain was so intense; I couldn't bring myself to get out of bed. All I could do was lie there and urinate on myself. After a couple of weeks of searching for something, anything, that would relieve the pain and allow me to rest, I realized the only time I was slightly less miserable was when I was in my recliner. The chair allowed me to prop myself up and support my neck and back while also reclining and relieving the pressure on the same. One evening I was too tired and in too much pain to get up and walk to the bedroom, and I ended up falling asleep in my recliner. The next morning I woke up feeling refreshed and rested. It was the first time I had slept for more than an hour since I returned home, and the difference in how I felt was incomparable. I immediately returned the cumbersome hospital bed and started sleeping in the living room in my recliner.

At the time of my release, I had not yet received approval from workers compensation to begin my outpatient treatment program at TIRR. The process took much longer than I expected. For two months I sat in my apartment, desperately wanting to return to therapy and continue working to regain as much strength and mobility as possible. The feelings of helplessness and being trapped in an impossible situation resurfaced. I hated not having control over my life or treatment plan. I was at the mercy of the insurance company, and there wasn't anything I could do about it. I was stuck in my house without the benefit of therapy until workers comp gave TIRR its approval. There was absolutely no benefit to sitting in my recliner all day, watching reruns and old movies. My emotional stability, as well as my physical condition, started to deteriorate. I was tired all the time, my muscles started to stiffen, walking and standing became more difficult, and muscle spasms became a constant. In addition to missing therapy, I missed the camaraderie I had felt while I was at TIRR. I had formed close relationships with the other patients, doctors, nurses, therapists, and other hospital staff. It was extremely difficult adjusting to the isolation and loneliness of being home alone for most of the day.

A typical day at home began with me spending a few moments with my son before he and his mother left for the day. I wasn't strong or well enough to care for myself, so keeping my son at home with me wasn't an option. Watching him leave was the saddest part of the day. I would start counting down the hours until he would return almost as soon as the door closed behind them. Shortly after they left, Ada, one of my two home health aides, would arrive. She came five days a week, Monday through Friday, but she didn't stay very long. Ada was responsible only for cleaning my surgical wounds and changing the bandages. She seemed like a nice lady, but she was in and out of the apartment so quickly that I never really got a chance to get to know her. After Ada left, I spent the next few hours sitting in my recliner and waiting for Hannah, the other nursing assistant, to arrive.

Typically there were premade meals either in the refrigerator or left out on the counter. If I wasn't in too much pain, I'd get up and eat breakfast and lunch, but there were quite a few days when I opted for the comfort of the recliner. It's hard to imagine a person being willing to be hungry when food is just a few feet away, but some days the pain of moving and walking was just too much to tolerate.

Hannah was also scheduled to come to my apartment Monday through Friday, and she usually arrived around four or five o'clock in the afternoon. She would help me take my medication and bring my lunch if I had not yet eaten it. She also helped me shower and get dressed for the evening. The worst part of her daily visits was the home bowel program. Just as the nurses had done in the hospital, Hannah would insert a suppository into my rectum and wait for me to have a bowel movement. If I was unable to "go" on my own, she would manually stimulate my bowels and remove the waste. It was just as uncomfortable and embarrassing as it had been in the hospital. After I was dressed and ready, Hannah would massage my neck and back, stretch my limbs, and set up my TENS unit. I was grateful to Hannah and everything she tried to do to make me as comfortable as possible, but it wasn't nearly as helpful and aggressive as the treatment I received at TIRR. I knew I needed to begin my outpatient treatment as soon as possible if I wanted to continue to get better. Hannah and I were usually finished for the day around six o'clock. She would help me back into my recliner before she left, and I would wait patiently for my baby boy to come home.

The monotony of doing the same thing every single day was depressing. The only bright spot was seeing my son's face light up as soon as our eyes met at the end of each day. Unfortunately, every other hour was filled with feelings of agony and defeat. It was difficult for me to come to grips with my depression, because there were times that it was masked by fleeting moments of happiness. I was on an emotional roller coaster, filled with extreme highs and the lowest of lows. Some days I stared at the ceiling, profusely thanking God I was alive. I was happy and relieved that I hadn't died alone in a ditch on the night of my accident. But within minutes, sometimes even seconds, I would be filled with feelings of sadness, emptiness, and despair. It was frustrating, because I knew I should be grateful to God for the many blessings He had given me, but I was also confused about why He would allow me to be in so much agony. I felt guilty for being so ungrateful, but no matter how hard I tried, I couldn't shake the depression.

Fortunately, before I was discharged from TIRR, my doctor noticed the changes in my mood and behavior and prescribed me a daily dose of Citalopram, an antidepressant. The Citalopram helped manage my depression, stabilized my emotions, and prevented the drastic mood swings, but it wasn't a quick fix or cure. Some mornings it was still very difficult to get out of bed and face a new day. When I experienced one of my bad days while I was at TIRR, I would ignore everything going on around me, block out my emotions, and use the negative thoughts and energy as motivation to push myself during my therapy sessions. That tactic worked while I was a patient at TIRR but proved entirely useless when I returned home.

I had no idea how much of a role my environment would have on my physical and emotional recovery. When I was living at TIRR, my days were filled with therapy, skills classes, and constant interaction with my family and friends, both old and new. I had the constant support of the other patients, doctors, and therapists. My entire support system was present and readily available to give me a word of encouragement or pat on the back when I was feeling too low to encourage myself. At TIRR I was so busy working to recover that I didn't have time to think about the past. But now that I was home, I had nothing but time to think about everything I had been and everything I'd lost. My apartment was filled with photographs and reminders of the life I had before my accident. I could hear the sounds of laughter that had once filled the strangely quiet rooms.

My apartment no longer felt like home. I felt just as confined and trapped as I had in the hospital. My son's mother and I were at a crossroads in our relationship, and the tension in the apartment was palpable. We weren't on the best terms, so I was uncomfortable asking her to help me. I struggled to function independently and be as self-sufficient as possible. I requested her assistance only when it was absolutely necessary. I tried to do everything on my own or wait for one of the nurses to come to help me. Frequently I would get frustrated, because it took me hours to do things that would take an able-bodied person only minutes to accomplish.

The weekends were the toughest, because the nurses came only during the week. On those days I would struggle to shower and dress myself. I remember being left alone in the shower, naked and cold, feeling completely vulnerable and powerless. I was at the mercy of others, and I hated it. I still needed help with almost everything. Once again I felt trapped. I was stuck inside a body that didn't work properly and in an unhealthy living situation that wasn't conducive to my recovery or happiness. I could feel myself unraveling, but I didn't know how to stop my emotions from spiraling out of control. A couple of weeks after I went home, I was at my lowest point. I was so tired of the physical and emotional pain that I was willing to do anything to make it go away.

During my darkest days when I was home alone, I thought about committing suicide. I was miserable and loathed every moment I had to spend at home. Nothing mattered anymore. I didn't care about being in a relationship, spending time with family and friends, or recovering from my injuries. I had several guns at my disposal and felt like ending my life was the only way to escape the pain and suffering. I didn't want to die, but I really wasn't living. I barely existed. I felt completely empty, devoid of all emotion, and felt like suicide was my only option. I wanted to be normal again, and since there was no chance of that happening, suicide seemed like the only logical resolution. I thought killing myself would alleviate all of my problems. I knew my family and friends, especially my son, would be devastated if I killed myself, but I hoped they would understand it was my only choice. I felt guilty and selfish, but I didn't think I had any other alternatives. Committing suicide was the only way I would be set free from a miserable life, an unhappy relationship, and a broken body. In death I could finally escape the depression that seemed to hunt me down no matter how hard I tried to hide from it.

I was also physically drained. I didn't have any more energy to spend on futile attempts to reclaim my old life. I was mentally, emotionally, and physically exhausted. I spent countless sleepless nights lying in my recliner, the only place that offered me some physical relief, quietly weeping because I felt I had nowhere to turn. I begged God for peace, but it seemed like my prayers were falling on deaf ears, because nothing changed. I felt like God had abandoned me again, because no matter how hard I prayed and pleaded with Him, I was still broken and depressed. Intellectually, I knew God wasn't going to give me a quick fix and that my recovery was going to be a very long and arduous process, but emotionally it was just too much for me to handle. Maybe I had taken a wrong turn to reach this dead end, but I didn't know what else to do but take my own life.

One morning I finally got the courage to do it. I decided that day would be the day I would end my life. I hadn't made any elaborate plans for how I was going to kill myself. I just knew I wanted the pain to stop. I slowly walked to the locked box to retrieve one of my handguns. When I picked it up, I was shocked at what I saw. Instead of looking at the barrel of the automatic weapon I was prepared to use to take my own life, I saw a reflection of my son's face. He was staring me in the eyes, willing me to live. What was I to do? Pull the trigger and leave my son fatherless?

How would anyone explain to Jadon years later that I had taken my own life? I was so overwhelmed that I put the gun down and cried for hours. Jadon was the only bright spot in an otherwise dreary existence. He was my sole motivation for living. Spending time with Jadon was the only time I felt remotely happy. But even during those times, the depression would creep in and infiltrate my thoughts. When I held my son, I often wondered if I'd ever be able to teach him to walk, run, and play sports. I was devastated at the thought that I might not be able to participate in normal father-and-son activities with him. I was also concerned about how I would provide for Jadon and myself. I knew I couldn't return to the police force, and as a disabled person my career options seemed limited at best. I knew it wasn't going to be easy, but I had to find a way to cope with my issues, adjust to my new reality, and live for myself and my son.

I finally decided to break my silence. I had no intention of talking to a psychiatrist or anyone else about what I was going through, but something had to give. I explained how I was feeling to my primary care physician, Dr. Berliner, and he referred me to Dr. Suzi Phelps, a psychologist. At first I was very apprehensive about meeting with her. I was embarrassed and didn't want anyone to think I was too weak to deal with my problems on my own, nor did I want them to think I was crazy. Besides, who could relate to what I was going through? But I was desperate and at rock bottom. The antidepressants weren't working, and I was spiraling deeper into my depression. I decided I had nothing to lose and made an appointment to meet with Dr. Phelps. I immediately felt a kinship with her, because she too lived with a disability. She had lost part of one of her legs in a boating accident. A piece of her life was missing and so was mine, but she was a survivor, and for the first time, I was speaking with someone who could actually relate to my personal struggles.

Dr. Phelps was extremely personable and I was comfortable

sharing my private thoughts and feelings with her. She started every session by offering me my favorite sour apple Jolly Rancher candy, which made me feel like she really cared about me. The majority of our hour long sessions were filled with me talking and venting. Her office was the only place I felt safe enough to communicate exactly how I felt. I could be candid with Dr. Phelps without the risk of being judged or condemned. We discussed both car accidents, my injuries, adjusting to my new life and my relationship with my son's mom. Dr. Phelps taught me how to control my emotions. She showed me how to use various coping strategies when I was confronted with frustrating situations at home and in therapy, instead of resorting to yelling and fighting. Dr. Phelps was literally a lifesaver. The opportunity to talk about my issues and receive positive feedback and realistic techniques I could use to deal with my daily stressors saved my life. By the time my sessions with Dr. Phelps ended, I had a new perspective on my life and recovery process. God had finally answered my prayers and given me the relief I so desperately needed.

I can happily report that I am no longer suffering from depression. I'm excited about the future and the plans God has in store for me. I have been to hell and back, and being on the other side gave me a greater appreciation for the "little" things we tend to take for granted. Every time I open my eyes, take a breath, or move my arms and legs, I thank God, because I know what it's like to be unable to do such simple things. I still encounter unexpected challenges and have moments of frustration and sadness, but I don't let negative thoughts or feelings consume me anymore. God restored my joy, and I refuse to let temporary circumstances in the natural world steal my peace. I hated being depressed, but it was also in my depression that I learned who I was and what I didn't want to become.

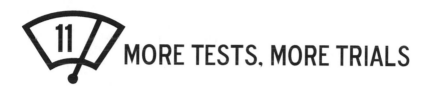

# MORE TESTS, MORE TRIALS

"They will fight against you, but will not overcome you, for I am with you and will rescue you," declares the Lord.

—Jeremiah 1:19

Two months after my release and several phone calls later, I finally received approval to begin outpatient therapy. My initial evaluation was done at the TIRR Kirby Glen Outpatient Therapy location. I was excited about beginning rehab but uncertain about what to expect. I'd heard the outpatient program was much more aggressive and knew the therapists were going to push me as far and as hard as possible. My body was still healing and I hadn't been to therapy in a couple of months, so I was unsure how much I could take. I was nervous about how my body would respond to the treatment, but I was determined to rise to the challenge. I wanted to prove to myself and everyone else that I could make a full recovery and eventually return to the police force, in spite of all the adversity I'd experienced as a result of my car accident. Time was of the essence. I had only a year from the date of my accident to return to work.

The initial evaluation consisted of several tests designed to measure my strength and range of motion in my upper and lower extremities. The test results would be used as a measuring stick to rate my progress, or regression, after I started my outpatient program. The evaluation also gave me the opportunity to set long- and short-term goals. I told the therapists my ultimate goal was to return to work as a police officer. Before beginning my outpatient treatment, I'd gone to the police academy and picked up all the materials I needed to be able to pass the Physical Training test. I presented the information to the therapists and explained that I wanted my physical therapy to be centered on the police academy's physical training requirements to ensure I would be able to go back to working the streets as a cop. The therapists conducting the initial exam were receptive to my requests and seemed resolute in helping me reach my goals. I was eager to begin therapy again; because I knew the sooner I started, the sooner I could get back to work.

I was under the impression that I would start my program immediately, so I was extremely disappointed to learn that it would be at least another few weeks before I could actually start. My heart sank when they told me how long I had to wait. I've always been taught that patience is a virtue, but I was tired of my patience being tested and tired of waiting. All I wanted to do was get better so I could work and provide for my family, and now I had to wait another month. I was frustrated and felt completely let down because I didn't have another moment to waste sitting at home. I'd already lost a lot of the progress I'd made before I was discharged from TIRR, and I knew I would continue to get worse if I didn't get back to therapy right away. If I didn't go to therapy, I couldn't get better. And if I didn't get better, I wouldn't be able to meet my recovery deadline. My colleagues were speculating about whether or not I'd be able to come back to work, and rumors were circulating around the department about my physical condition. Four months had already passed, which meant I had only eight months remaining before I had to make a permanent decision about my career. I wasn't physically able to meet the demands of police works, so I could either retire voluntarily or the police department would force me to retire. In the back of my mind I knew retirement was my only option, but I wanted to do it on my terms and in my time. I didn't want to be forced to leave the career I'd worked so hard to obtain.

My excitement and my hopes of returning to the police department started to dwindle as I sat at home waiting to return to therapy, but I refused to let negative thoughts infiltrate my mind and spirit. I decided to trust God and believe He was ordering my steps according to His divine plan for my life. It was time for me to replace my time line with God's will for my life. I knew His purpose and plan for my life would be far greater than any plan I could conceive for myself. I'd learned many lessons while I was confined to a hospital for all those weeks, not the least of which was patience. Before my accident, I'd spent my entire life running, always eager to move on to the next thing. I never took the time to fully appreciate all the "little things" I took for granted. Being forced to lie on my back, paralyzed and unable to care for myself, taught me that those "little things" were actually blessings and privileges that I should have cherished and respected. Now was the time for me to be patient and still and wait on the Lord.

Although I was firm in my faith and prepared for whatever God had in store for me, I couldn't help but wonder about what the next phase in my life would be like. If I wasn't going to be a police officer, then what was I going to do? How was I going to provide for my son? For the five years leading up to my car accident, my life had been consumed with police work. It was all I knew. Being a police officer was the most challenging yet rewarding experience of my lifetime. It was my dream job. I loved helping others and making a difference every day. I didn't know exactly what God had planned for me, but I was hopeful that whatever it was would allow me to continue to give back in a meaningful way. The Scripture says, "Many are the plans in a man's heart, but it is the Lord's purpose that prevails" (Proverbs 19:21). I meditated on those words every day. I accepted that I might not be able to return to work as police officer and understood that God's purpose for my life would exceed my greatest expectations.

Every day I sat home waiting to return to Kirby Glen was a test of my faith. In the natural, it seemed like the odds were stacked against me. My career as a police officer was hanging in the balance. Bills were pouring in, and I didn't have the financial resources to pay them. My body was deteriorating as I waited for the call letting me know I could begin outpatient therapy. And on top of everything else I was going through, I was still living in an unhappy, unfulfilling relationship. There were many days when it was difficult to remain steadfast in my faith. It wasn't always easy to look on the bright side when so many negative things were happening to me. Every time I took one step forward, something would happen (or not happen) that caused me to take two steps backward. I leaned heavily on my friends and family during this tough time. I was grateful to have such loyal, genuine people in my life. I didn't want to weigh them down with my personal problems, so I kept much of what I was going through to myself, but it was comforting to know they were there for me if I needed them.

Instead of confiding in man, I took my fears and concerns to God in prayer. I started to read my Bible daily and looked for answers in God's Word. I knew only He could give me the peace and security I needed to persevere against such tremendous odds. One of my favorite Bible verses, James 1:12, reads, "Blessed is the man who perseveres under trial because when he has stood the test, he will receive the crown of life that God has promised to those who love him." God hadn't failed me yet, so I continued to trust in Him. Instead of trying to do everything in my time and succumbing to the devil's tricks and schemes to deter my faith,

I resolved to wait on God's appointed time. I knew if I remained faithful, He would bring me through my storm and I would come out better than I was before it happened. If God was for me, then neither man nor the devil could come against me.

After a few weeks of waiting, I finally got the call telling me I could start outpatient therapy. I was thrilled to finally get started, but equally as anxious. Physically, I was much weaker than I was when I left TIRR. My left arm was completely useless and dangled lifelessly by my side. My left leg wasn't much better and caused me to walk much more slowly than usual. I couldn't turn my head from one side to the other. My neck was extremely stiff from the hardware, so I had to completely turn my entire body to look to the left or right. I was annoyed about the obvious regression in my physical condition, but there was no time to worry about things I couldn't control. I prepared myself to start over and do the work necessary to recover.

My first day at Kirby Glen brought back memories of when I trained as an athlete. As I walked into the rehabilitation center, I remembered how I had dreaded the grueling workouts I endured when I played sports. Back then, I was in the best shape of my life, but now I was barely able to move around. I wasn't training for a big game; I was fighting to regain some kind of normalcy in my life. I was still in an extreme amount of constant pain. Sometimes I had to put my hands in buckets filled with ice just to try to alleviate the burning sensation. It was torture, and some days I wanted to give up and quit. I had so far to go that it was hard to see the light at the end of the tunnel, but I knew I had to push past the pain.

The therapists at Kirby Glen were no nonsense. Ike, my occupational therapist, and Wendy, my physical therapist, were both relentless in their pursuits of a full recovery for me. They conducted their own assessments of my abilities and immediately started rigorous and aggressive courses of therapy. Wendy was very creative and used innovative techniques to push me in therapy. She was an athlete and related to my desire to want to get back to being normal. We spent countless hours on the treadmill, walking and jogging at different variations. We did several strengthening drills that incorporated the use of balance. One of the things she had me do was as simple as standing on one foot for thirty seconds. That may seem like an easy feat, but for me, it was difficult. It was another reminder that the simplest of things can be taken away from us at any minute and to never take those small things for granted again.

Shortly after I started working with her, Wendy noticed my left foot dragged the ground when I walked. She referred to it as a "foot drop," a disorder characterized by a patient's limited ability or inability to raise the foot at the ankle. It's typically caused by nerve injury, or a brain or spinal disorder. Wendy recommended I wear an ankle-foot orthosis brace to help improve my walking efficiency. The brace was uncomfortable, but eventually I got used to it. I wore it only at home and therapy because I was too embarrassed to wear a leg brace in public. I was still adjusting to living life with scars on my head and neck, as well as wearing a neck brace. Adding a leg brace was more than I could stand. I wore the brace for a few weeks and noticed tremendous improvement. The muscles in my ankle and foot were much stronger, and my gait was more comfortable and looked a lot more normal. Walking more normally was a huge accomplishment and motivated me to continue to work hard and get better.

I reached several milestones at Kirby Glenn. I jogged my first half mile there and eventually worked my way up to sprinting down the block. Every part of my body was responding to treatment, except my left arm. It still hung lifelessly by my side. Ike and I spent countless hours performing exercises to strengthen it, but none of them helped. We even tried the Armeo Spring machine, just like the one I used when I was a patient at TIRR, but it didn't help either. No matter how hard I tried, I couldn't get my left arm and hand to cooperate. I had to use my right hand to straighten out my left arm, and I couldn't turn my palm up or down. Holding a bottle of water in my left hand took an incredible amount of energy and was nearly impossible. I was pleased with my progress, but my left arm was a constant reminder of my limitations.

Ninety days after my accident, my neck had finally healed and I had an appointment with Dr. Schmitt, my neurosurgeon, to remove my cervical collar. I was super nervous about taking off the neck brace. It had been my security blanket for the last three months. Without it my neck would be exposed, and I had to trust that the titanium rods and screws were stable enough to keep my neck in place. I hadn't seen Dr. Schmitt since I'd been released from Memorial Hermann Hospital, so I was excited to show him how far I'd come. I wasn't surprised by the startled look on his face when he walked into the room. It was totally understandable, because the last time he'd seen me, I was lying flat on my back, unable to move, and battered and bruised from the accident. Dr. Schmitt stared at me in disbelief for a few seconds before he started scanning the room. When he asked me how I'd made it to his office, I realized he was looking around for my wheelchair. MaryAnn, my nurse case manager, was also in the room. I proudly told him I'd walked into his office on my own. His mouth dropped open, and he said he had not expected me to be doing so well so soon. I looked back at MaryAnn, and the only thing she could do was smile. He went on to explain that based on the extent of my injuries and the damage to my neck and back, he had never expected me to walk again.

The fact that a neurosurgeon was shocked by how much and how quickly I'd recovered was confirmation that I was a miracle. It solidified my belief that God was in control, and motivated me to continue to do my part to get better. I was nervous, but felt a sense of relief after he removed the collar from around my neck.

Wearing that brace the past three months was miserable. It was hot; it itched and caused me to sweat continuously, and as a result it developed a foul odor that I had to inhale constantly. My neck had decreased tremendously in size. It didn't look the same as it once did, and for the first time using a small mirror, I saw the long scar down the back. It was scary to look at, but it reminded me of how I blessed I was to have survived such a tragic ordeal. The X-rays showed how my neck was aligned by the screws and titanium rods. I must have counted over twenty screws alone. I didn't want to make any sudden moves, because I didn't trust that the hardware was stable enough to support my neck. Dr. Schmitt assured me that everything would be fine and even joked that my neck was sturdier than before. He said if I had any problems with anything to come back and see him. I was taking a new leap of faith as I walked out of his office into a world of uncertainty.

The clock was ticking, and I had only a few more months to make a final decision about my career. I had one year from the date of my injury to return to work; otherwise, I'd be forced to medically retire due solely on the fact that I couldn't physically perform the duties of a peace officer. I was making great strides in therapy, but it was still too early to know if I'd ever fully recover enough to resume working as a police officer. I received regular phone calls and letters from city representatives asking if and when I planned to return to work. The city's risk management department bombarded me with inquiries about my medical condition and physical status, but I could tell by the tone of the questions that they weren't genuinely concern about my health and well-being. It was heartbreaking to know that the city I'd given my life for could not care less about me. The reality of the situation was that while I was fighting for my life, they were concerned only with their financial bottom line. The city I'd worked so diligently to keep safe was denying me the financial benefits I'd earned and was entitled to as a disabled, medically retired police officer

I was only thirty-two years old at the time of my accident. The thought of retiring at such a young age was unfathomable. Nothing about early retirement was appealing to me. If I medically retired as a non-catastrophic claimant, I'd receive only 55 percent of my pension, which wasn't nearly enough to support myself and my son. How did they expect me to provide for my family? There was no way we could survive on half of my pension. The medical bills were mounting, and my other financial obligations had not stopped because I'd been injured. I tried to be optimistic about my recovery, but I knew I wouldn't be well enough to return to work in a few months. Even if I could eventually recover fully, it wasn't going to happen soon enough to meet the one-year deadline. I felt backed into a corner. I was drowning in debt and needed a lifeline. I was frustrated, saddened, and confused. I decided to reach out to the police officers' union for advice and support.

I scheduled a meeting with two of the union representatives so I could give them all the facts and get their feedback. I needed their advice and support. I was hopeful the situation would be resolved quickly and fairly, but just in case it wasn't, I didn't want to have to fight the city alone. I needed to know someone would have my back and advocate for my best interests. We started the meeting by discussing whether I could realistically return to work. J. J., one of the union reps, asked me if I really wanted to come back to the department as a police officer. I don't know why, but the question caught me off guard. Of course I wanted to be a cop again. I had never stopped thinking of myself as a police officer. I told him I really wanted to get back out there on the streets and that I was doing everything I could to get well so I could return to work.

The next question he asked was a game changer. He looked directly into my eyes and asked, "Do you think it's worth getting hurt again?" It's difficult to explain, but that was the first time I ever contemplated the possibility that I could get hurt again if I went to back to work. I sat quietly as he went on to say, "Jason, you've been through a lot in your life, including two major accidents that have nearly claimed your life. Have you ever stopped to think that maybe God is trying to tell you something? Maybe it's not meant for you to come back. Maybe He has something else greater for you to do on this earth." As I listened to them both encourage me to make whatever decision was best for me and my family, one of my favorite Scriptures popped into my head: "For I know the plans I have for you,' declares the Lord, 'plans to prosper you and not to harm you, plans to give you hope and a future." I hadn't had any intentions of making any decisions about my career when I met with them, but in that very moment I decided to medically retire. They were right. Returning to the police department wasn't worth risking my life. I'd accomplished more in my five years on the force than some officers achieve in their entire careers. I'd fulfilled my purpose as a police officer, and the Lord was calling me to do something different. It was time for me to close that chapter in my life, step out in faith, and trust God to provide for me and my family.

On May 18, 2012, I officially medically retired from the Houston Police Department. It was a bittersweet, emotional day. It wasn't easy turning in the badge and uniforms I'd worn so proudly for the last five years of my life. I said my farewells to the other officers in my unit, the command staff, and Chief McClelland. I was sad to leave my old life behind, but excited to start the next phase in my life.

After I retired, I was hopeful that the city of Houston would do the right thing and resolve my claim quickly and, most important, fairly. I was still focused on going to therapy and getting better. The last thing I wanted to do was get into a knock-down, drag-out fight with the city about my retirement and benefits. I didn't want any favors or special treatment. I simply wanted them to give me everything I'd earned and deserved. As a five-year veteran officer of the Houston Police Department, I had dedicated thousands of hours to protecting and serving the citizens of Houston, Texas.

Every time I put on my badge and uniform, I put my life on the line, without hesitation, to fulfill my oath of office and serve my community. I was horrified and hurt to learn that the loyalty and commitment I'd given to the city would not be reciprocated. Coming to grips with the fact that my injuries and paralysis would prevent me from returning to my lifelong dream job was devastating, but having to fight the very city I'd devoted my life to was upsetting and demoralizing. I'd sustained life-changing, paralyzing injuries in the line of duty that prevented me from returning to work and living a normal, active life. I was appalled and livid that the way the city chose to repay me was by denying me my benefits.

It took several months to resolve my workers' compensation claim. It was extremely physical and emotionally taxing. At the beginning of the long, arduous process, I was ordered to see a doctor chosen by the city to evaluate the severity of my injuries and provide his opinion of my eligibility for lifetime benefits. The entire doctor's visit took only ten or fifteen minutes. He didn't do a thorough examination. Instead, he skimmed my medical records, asked me a few basic questions about my medical history, conducted a very brief and basic exam, and sent me on my way. His initial opinion after the evaluation said that I met the criteria for lifetime benefits; however, after the city's private attorney asked him to review his original findings, he changed his opinion. In his subsequent report, he said I was medically but not legally qualified to receive lifetime benefits. A workers' compensation representative from the state issued a contrasting opinion that said I was qualified to receive lifetime benefits.

I didn't know what to think. What did he mean, "Medically but not legally qualified"? The attorney representing the city said the doctor's opinion held "presumptive weight" and denied the lifetime benefits. I was crushed. I did the only thing I could do, which was to immediately appeal the decision and wait for them to schedule a workers' compensation hearing to review my case.

In the midst of the process, I had a short but memorable conference call with the city attorney. I thought he might have a change of heart if I was able to explain my situation personally. He sat quietly as I pleaded my case and seemed unmoved by my story. I was confounded by his callous demeanor and asked him, "Would it have been better and easier if I had just died?"

He immediately responded in quite possibly the coldest tone I'd ever heard, "Mr. Roy, I'm not going to answer that, but what I will tell you is that I have a job to do and so do you." I was shocked by his response and insulted when he became silent after his remark. He treated me like a file and a case to be cleared, not like a police officer who'd sacrificed his body and nearly lost his life serving the community.

I was outraged, but I also felt powerless. I had the support of my union representative, but I didn't have the resources to fight the city. Shortly after the conference call, I decided to reach out to my contacts in the local media. Several local reporters had begun covering my story on the morning of my accident. I had kept in touch with a few of them and periodically provided them with updates on my health and the status of my workers' compensation case. The day after my call with the city attorney, I was interviewed by multiple local news outlets, and my story aired the same afternoon. It wasn't long after the interviews aired that the Houston Police Department union president was contacted by the mayor's office. The mayor personally said she was unaware of my situation and the issues I was having with regards to being approved for lifetime benefits. She issued a statement saying she did not support the decision to deny my benefits and asked the city attorney not to fight my lifetime benefits as a medically retired officer. A week later, I received a letter from the attorney expressing his agreement with the opinion of the state representative and approval of my lifetime benefits.

 **ALL ALONE**

Be joyful always, pray continually; give thanks in all circumstances, for this is God's will for you in Christ Jesus.

1 Thessalonians 5:16–18

There are no words to adequately convey the devastation I felt when I could no longer provide and care for my son. Being awarded benefits offered some relief because at least I knew I would be able to meet my financial obligations as a parent, but I was still worried about my ability to actively participate in the physical aspect of raising him. As a parent, I was instinctively more concerned about how my spinal cord injuries would affect his life than how they would affect my own. Initially I just wanted to survive so I could be a part of his life in whatever capacity possible. But as I slowly began to recover from my nearly fatal injuries, I became more concerned about the quality of my parenting. Caring for an infant when I was able-bodied was difficult, so I was overwhelmed by the thought of raising my son with my disabilities. When I first returned home from the hospital, I wasn't strong enough to do much other than hold him while I sat in my recliner. I wanted to help his mom care for him, but I couldn't.

I couldn't change his diapers, bathe him, or even pick him up to comfort him when he was crying. I was adjusting to living life with one hand and could barely walk from one room to the next. I was afraid I'd drop him if I tried to pick him up on my own. I was still learning to care for myself again, and didn't know how I'd manage to take care of my son too.

A few months after I came home from TIRR, my son's mother and I agreed it was best for us to separate and co-parent our son from separate homes. Separating from Jadon's mother was one of the most difficult decisions of my life. My entire world revolved around my son. From the moment I learned I would be a father, everything I did was for him. Knowing I wouldn't get to see him and hold him every day tore me apart. It broke my heart that I wouldn't be able to wake up to his smile and feel his little hands gripping my neck every day. I wrestled with my decision for weeks, but I knew it was the right choice. My son deserves to have two healthy, happy parents—loving parents—even if it means we have to live apart. God gave me peace about my decision, and I trusted He would protect my son in my absence.

After I got past the pain of living without Jadon, I started to feel the pressure of being a single father. I was not only single, but disabled. I didn't know how I was going to care for an infant on my own, but I knew I was going to have to figure it out. He was my responsibility. It was my job to raise him, and I refused to let my physical limitations rob me of the privilege of being a father to my son. I was blessed to have the support of my friends and family, but I was determined to learn to take care of him on my own. Initially I leaned on my parents a lot. Whenever Jadon was in my custody, they came over and helped me with the more physically demanding chores, such as bathing him, changing his diapers, dressing him, and lifting him into his car seat and high chair. I was appreciative of their willingness to help, but sometimes I got frustrated because I couldn't do more by myself. I wanted to take care of his needs. I didn't like feeling helpless, nor did I want to have to depend on other people to help me take care of my son. Eventually I realized I could either continue to try to be a "normal" parent or I could just be the best parent I could be. I had to learn to work within my limitations and make adjustments that allowed me to care for my son to the best of my ability.

Time management has been one of the major keys to being a successful single parent. Because it takes me longer to accomplish most physical tasks, I always give myself more than enough time to get things done. Jadon and I are both on very strict schedules. Of course there are occasional unexpected issues, but we typically follow the same routine. We don't venture out to many places outside my comfort zone. I prefer to spend high-quality time at home, so I purposely built my house in a kid-friendly, planned community. Everything we need, including parks, pools, stores, and restaurants, are only minutes away.

I try to participate in as many sports activities as I can with him, but there are definitely limits to what I can do. He is a ball of energy, and there are times when I just can't keep up with him. Sometimes I get frustrated when I have to stop playing a game or chasing him around the yard or playground because I have a muscle spasm in my back or neck. I hate the look of disappointment on his face when I tell him I need to take a break. But I am grateful I'm alive and able to do as much as I can. I've accepted that I may not ever be able to physically do as much as other parents, but I've promised my son I'll die trying to be the best father I can be.

# VICTORY

Then the Lord said: "I am making a covenant with you. Before all your people I will do wonders never seen before done in any nation in all the world. The people you live among will see how awesome is the work that I, the Lord, will do for you."

—Exodus 34:10

After five months of intense outpatient therapy, I was discharged from TIRR's Kirby Glen location and transferred to Spero Rehab. Spero is the Latin word for "hope" or "to hope for." The name is appropriate because everyone at Spero is dedicated to restoring hope in their patients' lives, and I was hopeful I would make a full recovery. I'd made significant progress at TIRR, but there was still a lot more work to be done. While I was waiting in the lobby, I ran into Damian, my old roommate from TIRR. I hadn't seen him in more than six months. We chatted for a few minutes until it was time for me to meet with the therapists. We'd bonded while we were at TIRR, and I was excited to reconnect with him. This time around, I was going to make sure we didn't lose contact with each other again.

My first day at Spero was filled with the typical paperwork

and exams I'd become accustomed to since my accident. As usual, the first order of business was the initial evaluation, which was similar to the preliminary assessment I'd had when I first arrived at Kirby Glen. The therapist conducting the evaluation took lots of measurements of nearly every part of my body and asked questions about my overall physical condition. After the exam was complete, we discussed my expectations and developed a clear, concise list of goals. My outpatient program at Spero consisted of three two-hour sessions each week. Each session was broken down into one hour of physical therapy and one hour of occupational therapy.

My initial impression of the staff and therapists was that they were kind, compassionate, and dedicated. I was looking forward to working with them and taking advantage of everything they had to offer. Spero was much smaller than the expansive Kirby Glen facility; however, it is a premier rehabilitation clinic, and I knew I'd receive top-notch treatment. In spite of its size, it had all the essential machines, including a Hydroworx therapy pool similar to the ones used by professional athletes. My primary concern was my left arm. It still wasn't functioning properly and was extremely weak. I was hopeful the therapists at Spero would have some new and innovative techniques to help rehabilitate and strengthen it.

On my road to recovery, I've met a lot of influential people, but none like Katie, Spero's Clinical Director and an occupational therapist, and Jonathan, a young and energetic physical therapist. These two were the most memorable. Katie is one of the most kindhearted people I've ever encountered in my life. From the moment I met her, I knew she was genuinely concerned about my total recovery. She was as passionate about helping me regain my mental and emotional stability as she was about restoring my physical health. Katie never treated me like just another patient or an insurance claim; she made me feel like a priority. I've always been very guarded, so I was shocked at how comfortable

I felt confiding in her. I was going through a host of personal and professional issues when I started at Spero, and Katie was a constant source of support. She was never too busy to listen or hesitant to offer her assistance.

In addition to being very sensitive to her patients' needs and extraordinarily emotionally supportive, Katie is one of the best occupational therapists in the business. She was aggressive but gentle. She spent countless hours working on my arm, hand, and neck, using cutting-edge technology and groundbreaking therapeutic techniques to help relieve the pain. One such device Katie and the other therapists used was the Dolphin Neurostim. The Dolphin Neurostim uses minute micro current impulses to gently relax muscles, calm the nervous system, and release endorphins. The direct electrical current normalizes neuroactivity throughout the body. It wasn't a painful process. The currents felt like needle pricks, but nothing ever actually penetrates through the skin. It didn't completely eliminate the pain, but it did give me some relief.

Katie also introduced me to the Hydroworx pool. I loved working out in the pool. It allowed me to perform exercises I couldn't do on land because almost all of my bodyweight was eliminated when I was in the water. Working out in the pool provided immediate results and helped improve my overall balance, range of motion, and strength. Katie's compassionate nature, generous spirit, and impeccable leadership skills have helped her create more than just a rehabilitation clinic; Spero is a family. Her dedication to the patients' complete health is evidenced by her willingness to extend and sometimes overextend her time, knowledge, and resources to ensure everyone who comes through Spero's doors receives exceptional patient care. Katie and her staff have helped me regain my physical strength, but more important, they've helped restore my hope and my faith in people.

Jonathan is one of the liveliest and most innovative therapists

I know. He is extremely knowledgeable and passionate about his profession and takes physical therapy to the next level. Jonathan was exceedingly empathetic to my situation. He made me feel like he understood my condition from my personal perspective. Jonathan communicated with me in a way that made me feel as if he identified with my emotions and struggles, but not like he pitied or felt sorry for me. He taught me not to diminish my accomplishments. I was so focused on rehabbing the parts of my body that didn't work, I didn't acknowledge how far I'd come in my recovery. I hadn't truly taken the time to appreciate how miraculous it was that I was alive, much less walking on my own. Although I was still as determined as ever to get better, I took Jonathan's advice and embraced my body as it was. I realized I didn't have to wait until I was 100 percent to start living and enjoying life again. What if I never regained full functionality of my left arm and leg? Was I going to let that deter me from living a full, active life? Absolutely not!

Jonathan was firm but always encouraging. He pushed me beyond my limits and motivated me to go further than I thought I could. I was noticeably stronger and in better overall physical shape after several weeks of rehabbing at Spero. I even noticed improvement in my left hand and arm. The things he was able to get my body to do were mind blowing. I was grateful for how well my body was responding to the treatment and felt like there were no limits to how far I could go. That is, until Jonathan suggested I run in a 5k race. I thought he had gone completely insane. I was intrigued by the idea of running in a race, but couldn't fathom actually doing it. I didn't think my legs were strong enough, nor was I sure I had the stamina to run three miles. He was relentless in his pursuit to get me to agree to run in the race. Every time I saw him, he asked me if I'd changed my mind, and each time I said no. After a couple of weeks of him asking persistently, I finally got the courage to do it. By the time I agreed, the race was only three weeks away, and there wasn't much time to prepare.

Jonathan and I quickly adjusted my therapy regimen and immediately started training for the run. I had to get acclimated to running outside, so we spent the majority of my therapy sessions running outside. We had to make sure I was prepared, but didn't want to do too much too quickly. We eased into it and started with short jogs around the facility's parking lot. My first jog around the lot was only about a hundred yards, but it may as well have been a hundred miles. It was a definite eye-opener and showed me I wasn't nearly in as good a shape as I'd thought. We incorporated more cardio exercises into my workout routine, and I started exercising and walking outside of my therapy sessions. Each time I went for a jog, I increased the distance and pushed myself to beat my previous time. I also stopped running in the parking lot and started jogging in the streets in an effort to get my feet used to the uneven, hard pavement I would be running on during the race. I worked out and trained hard until the very last minute.

I was a bundle of nerves on the day of the race. Thankfully, I wasn't alone. The entire Spero staff and a few other patients ran in the race and were by my side every step of the way. I was overwhelmed by their support and faith in me. I had to stop to catch my breath a few times, but I managed to complete the 5k in forty-six minutes. I was overjoyed when I finished. Sweat and tears rolled down my face. I was in awe of God's greatness. God had performed yet another miracle in my life. He gave me the physical strength and mental fortitude to accomplish something I never imagined I could do. Philippians 4:13 reads, "I can do all things through Christ who strengthens me." I was proud of my accomplishment, but I knew it was God's grace and mercy that carried me across the finish line that day.

*Jason running with Therapist Jonathan at his first 5k marathon*

# 14 MORE ADJUSTMENTS

I have been crucified with Christ and I no longer
live, but Christ lives in me. The life I live in the body,
I live by faith in the Son of God, who loved me and
gave himself for me.

—Galatians 2:20

Successfully completing the race gave me the confidence boost I needed to begin living a full, active life in spite of my physical challenges. I'd been so consumed with "getting my old life back," I hadn't realized how much of my current life I was wasting. I'd never considered myself a vain person, but I eventually came to understand that much of my confidence and identity had been directly related to my physical strength and outward appearance. As an athlete and police officer, I had to be strong, tough, and at times intimidating. Physical fitness had been a huge part of my life since early childhood, so losing my ability to walk, run, and exercise as swiftly and intensely as I had before my spinal cord injury made me feel incomplete. It was difficult going from such an active lifestyle to barely being able to move around and being in constant pain.

I felt like a part of me had died in my police car. But thank

139

God Jonathan forced me to run in the race with him, because it gave me that extra push I needed to regain my confidence in myself and accept my new body, my new scars, and my new life. I started to wear my scars and physical imperfections as badges of honor. I no longer viewed them as disfigurements; they were physical reminders of not only my journey and struggles, but also of God's goodness and mercy. It was better to be alive with flaws than the alternative. The moment I crossed the finish line, I made a conscious decision to make the most of every minute of every day. I knew the mental scars wouldn't evaporate overnight, but I was hopeful my new outlook on life would make facing the difficult moments a little easier.

There was an immediate shift in my attitude and behavior after I completed the race. I stopped focusing so much energy on fixing my body and started adjusting my environment to meet my needs. I realized it was time for me to accept where I was in my recovery and adapt. I wasn't giving up on making a full recovery, but I didn't want to squander another moment living in the past or waiting on the future. It was time for me to live in the moment. I stopped getting frustrated by the daily obstacles I encountered, and started channeling my energy into finding solutions and alternatives.

Getting dressed was one of the most difficult challenges after my spinal cord injury. My occupational therapists were phenomenal in helping me increase my functional independence. They taught me to take care of my personal hygiene and grooming needs, feed myself, and perform most of my daily living tasks independently, but I had never had the opportunity to learn to dress myself. While I was a patient at TIRR, there was always a nurse or family member available to help me get dressed for the day. In therapy I practiced various techniques for putting on and removing shirts and pants, but I was never forced to actually do it on my own. As a result, when I got home and needed to dress myself, I couldn't. The lack of mobility in my left arm made it nearly impossible. The first several times I tried using the methods I learned in therapy, the shirt got stuck on the top of my head. I finally managed to get it over my head a few times, but my success was short-lived because I still couldn't get it past my neck. It was maddening and caused me to forgo participating in activities such as social functions and attending church. I was grateful for the things I learned in therapy, but I had to figure out ways of doing things that worked for me.

Early one Sunday morning, I walked into my closet and picked out a T-shirt, a pair of jeans, and some sneakers. I was determined to do whatever it took to dress myself so I could go to church. I was fed up with being held hostage by my inability to put on a shirt and pair of pants, and literally took matters into my own hands. Since my left arm and hand were virtually useless, I had to figure out a way to dress myself with only my right hand. Church didn't start until 11:00 a.m., but I started preparing at the crack of dawn to make sure I had enough time to get ready.

I tried several different ways of putting on my shirt, until I finally stumbled upon a method that worked for me. It was unlike anything I'd learned in therapy, but it seemed to work perfectly. I used my right hand to put the shirt over my head. Once it was over my head, I grabbed the middle part of the shirt near the collar and pulled it down until I could maneuver it over my left hand and arm. After my left arm was through the left sleeve of the shirt, I used my right arm to pull it down in the back and slide my right arm through the right sleeve. It took me a while to master it, but after several weeks of practicing, it became a part of my normal routine.

Putting on my shirt was a major achievement, but it was only half the battle. I still needed to get my pants on and my belt through the loops and buckled. Putting on shorts didn't present too much of an issue, but getting my legs through narrow pants legs was much more difficult than I expected. It took a great deal of energy just to hold up the right side of my pants with my right hand while struggling to put my left leg through the pants leg. Additionally, I couldn't bend my foot at the ankle to make it easily fit through the pants legs, so frequently it got stuck, forcing me to start the tiresome process all over again. It took several attempts and a handful of falls before I got my pants on, but I did it.

Unfortunately, it wasn't until I had my pants on that I realized I couldn't put my belt on with one hand. I remember standing in the bathroom feeling completely deflated. I felt like everything I'd accomplished in the last two hours was meaningless now that I couldn't get my belt on and buckled. I considered not wearing a belt at all, but my pants were much too loose around the waist for that to be a viable option. Just as I was about to quit and get back in bed, it dawned on me that I should have put the belt through the loops first. I was a bit discouraged that I had to start all over, but I was excited I'd figured it out on my own. Forty-five minutes later, I was dressed and ready to go to church!

# BACK IN CHURCH

> And when you stand praying, if you hold anything against anyone, forgive him, so that your father in heaven may forgive you your sins.
>
> —Mark 11:25

I could feel the presence of the Lord as soon as I walked through the doors of the church. The music was blaring and the congregation was on its feet, singing and dancing during the praise and worship part of service. I hadn't been able to attend church in the nine months since my accident. I'd spent a lot of time praying and watching church on television, but I longed for the comfort, peace, and security I felt when I was actually in the Lord's house.

Everything at Lakewood Church was just as I remembered it. Pastor Joel's face was still lighted with his vibrant smile, and his wife, Victoria, was as inspiring and energetic as ever. There were friendly greeters stationed at every door and helpful ushers available to escort members and visitors to their seats. Normally I would have sat near the front of the church, but that day I chose a seat in the back, near an exit. I wasn't completely healed and couldn't walk as fast as I could before my accident. I didn't want to get in anyone's way or get caught in too much traffic on my way out. I wanted to join in the praise and worship, but I didn't have the strength to stand for long periods. After I made my way to my seat, I spent a few moments just taking it all in. It felt good to be home.

I was glad to be back in church, but my heart was heavy. For most of my life I had battled with forgiving others and letting go of grudges. I'd made some progress in the preceding years, but my accident caused a major setback. I was filled with rage and had not forgiven the suspect who led me on the high-speed chase that forever changed my life. I blamed him for every negative thing that happened as a result of the accident. I blamed him for my injuries, my pain, and the loss of the career I had worked so hard to obtain. *Hate* is a strong word I almost never use, but sometimes my anger and disdain for him felt like hatred. I also resented that my partner walked away from the accident with only a few minor bumps and bruises. Of course I was thankful he wasn't injured, but I was confused about why God had chosen me to endure such trauma and pain. I didn't understand why God allowed him to come out unscathed but left me barely clinging to life. Every day I found myself having flashbacks of the accident. I pictured the police car flying through the air and saw myself bloody and battered. My memories seemed so real that I could feel the force of impact when we landed in the ditch and the awful smell of fumes from the car. Every time I thought about that night, the feelings of terror returned with a vengeance.

I didn't like being angry, bitter, and resentful. It was emotionally and spiritually unhealthy, and was also taking a toll on my physical health. The stress of carrying around so much emotional baggage was preventing me from living my best life. As a faithful Christian, I knew I had to forgive those people before I could move forward with my life. I knew their sins were no greater than mine. God had forgiven me and sacrificed His Son to pay the debt for my sins, so who was I to withhold my forgiveness? I knew what I needed to do; I just didn't know how to do it. I was hopeful I'd find the answers and strength I needed to deliver myself from the spiritual bondage that had taken over me.

Bishop T. D. Jakes was the guest speaker that particular Sunday. I almost fell out of my seat when he started preaching a sermon on forgiveness. It was a divine moment, and I knew that day had been planned and orchestrated by God. It wasn't a coincidence that after weeks of feeling too discouraged to come to church, I had chosen to come on the day Bishop Jakes preached a sermon about forgiveness. Everything about the service, from the choir's song selection to the sermon, was exactly what I needed to hear. I'm paraphrasing, but Bishop Jakes said that unforgiveness is when one's spirit gets stuck in a state of pain from which it cannot eradicate itself. When he spoke those words, I felt like everyone else in the room disappeared and he was talking directly to me. His words immediately resonated in my mind and heart. I'd allowed myself to get stuck in my anger. I couldn't see past my hurt, rage, and pain. I was holding on to past events I could neither control nor change. I realized that the only person I was punishing by refusing to forgive was me. The hatred and resentment I harbored in my heart was blocking my blessings and causing me to drift further and further away from my destiny. I realized I would never be able to position myself to fulfill God's will for my life if I didn't forgive and let go of the past.

I was overcome with emotion in the midst of listening to Bishop Jakes's sermon. Tears streamed down my face as I opened my heart and forgave everyone I felt had wronged me. I asked God to come into my heart, forgive me for my sins, and give me the strength to accept my new normal and live in peace. When I opened my eyes, I felt like the weight of the world had been lifted off my shoulders. I felt free.

# FROM ZERO 2 A HUNDRED

> I thank Christ Jesus our Lord, who has given me strength, that He considered me faithful, appointing me to His service. Even though I was once a blasphemer and a persecutor and a violent man, I was shown mercy because I acted in ignorance and unbelief. The grace of our Lord was poured out on me abundantly, along with the faith and love that are in Christ Jesus.
>
> —1 Timothy 1:12–14

Returning to church was the first step in my new spiritual beginning. I had devoted the last several months to rebuilding my physical body, and I was long overdue for a spiritual overhaul. After my accident and spinal cord injury, I felt like a broken man. I thought regaining my physical strength would make me feel whole again, but even as my wounds started to heal and my broken bones began to mend, I felt incomplete. I was grateful to be alive and thankful for all the blessings God had given me, but something was still missing. I knew God had spared my life because He had a purpose for me, but something was holding me back from rising to my full potential. I wasn't sure what it was or how to overcome it, but my faith and spiritual foundation led me back to the church.

JASON ROY

I started attending Sunday church services regularly and reading my Bible on a more consistent basis. The more I went to church, the more I began to crave the word of God. I loved being in His presence and worshiping and fellowshipping with other Christians so much that I started attending midweek services and participating in the men's ministry. Every time I left Lakewood, I felt reenergized, self-assured, blessed, and triumphant. The words from Pastor Joel's sermons were taking root in my heart and spirit. I started to believe I was a child of the Most High God. I received that I was a victor and not a victim. I accepted that as a Christian and a believer, I had God's unprecedented favor and could do all things through Christ who strengthened me. I could feel my confidence and my faith growing simultaneously, but there was still something nagging at my spirit.

Pastor Joel and the associate ministers at Lakewood closed every service and meeting with an invitation to accept Christ as one's Lord and Savior. There were a few times when I thought about standing, but I had accepted Christ as a child and had been saved for most of my life. I wasn't embarrassed; I just didn't think the invitation applied to me. But every time I heard the words *or maybe you've grown cold toward God,* I felt something stir in my spirit. After several months of ignoring my gut feeling, I decided to take a leap of faith and rededicated my life to Christ. The moment I stood up and recited the salvation prayer, I felt born again. I asked God to come into my heart, forgive me of my sins, and wash me clean. It was such a relief to know God was so loving and forgiving that He'd wipe the slate clean after just one meaningful prayer. God didn't require me to list all of my wrongs or publicly apologize to those I had offended. He simply accepted me as I was, forgave me, and gave me yet another chance to live my life according to His will. I was in awe of God's goodness and mercy. I decided in that moment that I wanted to live a life pleasing to Him.

Renewing my commitment to Christ and atoning for my sins allowed God to begin to work and move in my life. The negative thoughts and sin that had previously filled my mind and heart were preventing me from maturing in my spirituality and growing closer to God. After I let go of all the pain and baggage from the past, I was finally able to receive and accept God's calling on my life. I started to realize that everything that had happened to me, from birth until the moment I completely submitted myself to God's will, was part of His divine plan for my life.

Nothing I've endured or witnessed has been an accident. My steps were ordered by the Lord to prepare me for my ultimate purpose. In the natural, I should not have survived the car accident in 1994. I was pronounced dead at the scene and left covered with a sheet in the middle of a busy intersection, but God decided it was not my time to go. He shielded my body from the oncoming traffic and used a dream to wake a sleeping stranger and send him to my aid. Seventeen years later, I should have died in yet another tragic car accident, but once again, that was not God's plan for my life. He saved my life and built me up from a shell of my former self so I could use my testimony to glorify His name.

I can witness to others about God's grace and mercy because I have been the recipient of it at the highest level. I can testify that He can and will perform miracles in your life, because I am a living example of His miraculous power. I have suffered unimaginable loss, so I know how to be compassionate. I've endured extreme sadness and depression, so I have a greater appreciation for happiness and joy. I have learned to live with my physical disabilities and limitations, so I know God will always give you what you need to survive.

I've always known I wanted to leave my mark on the world. For many years I thought it would be as an all-star baseball player. Later in life, I decided to pursue a career in law enforcement, hoping that as a police officer, I could change the world by putting away one bad guy at a time. Now I know God has called me to use my story to encourage others and testify about His greatness on a global level. In spite of the literal blood, sweat, and tears I endured, I survived. God's grace and mercy kept me in my darkest hours. I am not ashamed of the things I've been through in my life. God chose me to carry out a very special assignment. I am proud that I had the strength to overcome every tragedy and obstacle I've faced in my lifetime. I am appreciative of the lessons I've learned through my adversity. The hardships I've encountered have made me a better Christian man, father, son, brother, and friend. I have a greater appreciation for life and a new respect for time. I truly understand that tomorrow is not promised. I'm committed to maximizing each moment and being a living example for my brothers and sisters in Christ. I'm blessed and honored that God chose me to be a living testimony. It is my duty and responsibility to use my journey as a tool to inspire others and draw them closer to God. God has taken me from zero to one hundred, and I want you to have faith that He can and will do the same for you.

If you have not accepted Jesus Christ as your personal savior, I want to close this book by inviting you to pray this simple prayer, the prayer of salvation:

> Dear God in heaven, I come to you in the name of Jesus. I acknowledge to you that I am a sinner, and I am sorry for my sins and the life that I have lived; I need your forgiveness.
>
> I believe that your only begotten Son, Jesus Christ, shed His precious blood on the cross at Calvary and died for my sins, and I am now willing to turn from my sin. You said in Your Holy Word, Romans 10:9 that if we confess the Lord our God and believe in our hearts that God raised Jesus from the dead, we shall be saved. Right now

I confess Jesus as the Lord of my soul. With my heart, I believe that God raised Jesus from the dead. This very moment I accept Jesus Christ as my own personal Savior and according to His Word, right now I am saved. Thank You, Jesus, for your unlimited grace which has saved me from my sins. I thank You, Jesus that your grace never leads to license but rather it always leads to repentance. Therefore Lord Jesus transform my life so that I may bring glory and honor to you alone and not to myself.

Thank You, Jesus, for dying for me and giving me eternal life, Amen.

# THE ZERO 2 A HUNDRED FOUNDATION

The Zero 2 a Hundred Foundation was inspired and established by Jason Roy in 2013. The foundation is dedicated to improving the quality of life of children and adolescents suffering from brain and/or spinal cord injuries by providing financial resources and information to ensure they receive the high quality rehabilitative treatment necessary to maximize their ability to function and live as independently as possible.

The foundation aims to provide financial assistance for rehabilitative treatment for children and adolescents with brain and/or spinal cord injuries who have exhausted their financial resources and as a result are unable to receive the therapeutic treatment they desperately need. To receive financial awards, candidates must (1) be between four and twenty-one years of age, (2) have suffered either a brain or spinal cord injury, and (3) exhibit financial need.

The vision of the foundation is to show children and adolescents with brain and spinal cord injuries that there is still hope to live.

# ACKNOWLEDGMENTS

First, a thank you to my Lord and Savior for sparing my life and trusting me with this awesome responsibility of sharing my testimony to glorify Him and inspire others.

Thank you to my precious son, Jadon Isaiah Roy. Son, I love you more than you will ever know. You were, and continue to be, my motivation to live and are God's greatest and most perfect gift. Thank you to my beautiful mother, Ollie Roy, who gave me life and continuously offers her undying love and support, and my incredible father, Leonard Roy, who has been faithfully by my side my entire life. Dad, thank you for your unconditional love, support, and guidance. Thank you to my wonderful family, especially my sister, Lisa Roy, Aunt Ann, Robert and Jessica Vermont, Keith Roy Sr., Keith Roy Jr., Sam Roy Jr., Mama Roy, CeCe Roy, Devin Lancellin, Rose Roy, Loren Williams, Uncle Kurtis and Aunt Anne, and a host of other loving family members.

I'm so grateful to my loyal and genuine friends who have weathered this storm with me. It has been a long and difficult journey, and you guys have been by my side every step of the way. You are more than friends; you're family!

This book would not have been possible without the support and encouragement of my family, friends, physicians, colleagues, fellow Houstonians, and the countless strangers who have offered their prayers and concern. I also want to acknowledge the local media and news stations that told my story and advocated for me, with a special thank you to Rucks Russell, Joel Isenbaum, Andy Cerota, and Isaiah Carey.

Thank you to all of my colleagues at the Houston police and fire departments, specifically my partner, Gerald Meola, who was by my side on the night of our accident; the men and women of HFD Station 55 and Officer Diego Morelli for their heroic efforts to keep me safe and alive; Lieutenant Steve Casko for his incredible support; and the numerous officers who unselfishly donated blood on my behalf.

I offer my sincerest gratitude to Houston Police Chief Charles McClelland and Mayor Annise Parker for their continued support and prayers; Rhonda Childree and Sandy Gosnell, my case manager and adjuster, for their hard work and dedication to my case; Victor Hung and the officers who assisted in hosting and facilitating an awesome benefit on my behalf; and Mike Mitchell of Texas Police Trust, Rick Hartley of the 100 Club, Renee Cravens of Assist the Officer; and Ray Hunt, Doug Griffith, J. J. Berry, and Krystal LaReau of the Houston Police Officers Union for their generous support and financial assistance.

I wouldn't be here to tell my story if it were not for the talented team of medical professionals from Memorial Hermann Hospital, TIRR, and Spero Rehabilitation Facility, who treated and cared for me during every stage of my treatment and recovery. I offer my most heartfelt thanks for your individual and collective efforts to keep me living day in and day out. Special thanks to Dr. Karl Schmidt and his gifted team of surgeons for repairing my broken body; Dr. Jeffrey Berliner for his unyielding support and guidance; and all of the physical and occupational therapists who continue to work tirelessly with me. I would not have made it this far without each of you.

Last but not least, I would like to thank Pastors Joel and

Victoria Osteen and John Gray of Lakewood church for their continued inspiration and motivation each and every Sunday.

I ask for the forgiveness of all those who have been with me throughout the years whose names I didn't mention. Your contributions are greatly appreciated, and I love you with all my heart.